AYAAN HIRSI ALI was born in Somalia, was raised Muslim, and spent her childhood and young adulthood in Africa and Saudi Arabia. In 1992, Hirsi Ali came to the Netherlands as a refugee, escaping a forced marriage to a distant cousin she had never met. She learned Dutch and worked as an interpreter in abortion clinics and shelters for battered women. After earning her college degree in political science, she worked for the Labor Party. She denounced Islam after the September 11 terrorist attacks and now works as a Dutch parliamentarian, fighting for the rights of Muslim women in Europe, the enlightenment of Islam, and security in the West.

Further praise for *The Caged Virgin*:

'*The Caged Virgin* is intensely felt, and filled

Observer

'The author of *The Cage*   political
correctness . . . This is a   ulness and
bravery. In her angry cla   she is not afraid to
question some of the most   ets of Islam . . . What Islam
needs, she feels, is a swift dose of 18th-century enlightenment – it's
time to put down the Koran and pick up Voltaire . . . She writes with
passion, with burning indignation . . . Everyone who cares about
the systematic and legalized oppression of women should study this
powerful cry for reason'

Kate Saunders, *Sunday Times*

'While Hirsi Ali never holds back in her criticism of Islam, she has
valid and important recommendations about improving the plight of
abused Muslim women. Tackling one of the most sensitive issues of
our time with provocative and passionate arguments, *The Caged
Virgin* is, above all else, a brave book'

Irish Times

THE CAGED VIRGIN

A Muslim Woman's
Cry for Reason

Ayaan Hirsi Ali

POCKET
BOOKS

LONDON • SYDNEY • NEW YORK • TORONTO

First published in Great Britain by The Free Press in 2006
This edition first published by Pocket Books in 2007
An imprint of Simon & Schuster UK Ltd
A CBS COMPANY

Originally published in The Netherlands in 2004 as
De Maagdenkooi by Uitgeverij Augustus (Amstel Publishers, b.v.)

Published by arrangement with Ayaan Hirsi Ali and Uitgeverij Augustus,
part of Amstel Publishers, b.v.

9 10

Simon & Schuster UK Ltd
1st Floor
222 Gray's Inn Road
London WC1X 8HB

www.simonsays.co.uk

Simon & Schuster Australia
Sydney

A CIP catalogue record for this book is available from the British Library.

ISBN-13:978-1-4165-2623-0

Printed and bound in Great Britain by
CPI Cox & Wyman, Reading, RG1 8EX

Designed by Joseph Rutt

With grateful acknowledgment to the Foundation for the Production and
Translation of Dutch Literature for their kind assistance

To the spirit of liberty

Contents

Preface

Breaking Through the Islamic Curtain

The attacks on the United States of September 11, 2001, prompted the West to launch a massive appeal to Muslims around the world to reflect on their religion and culture. American President George W. Bush, British Prime Minister Tony Blair, and numerous other leaders in the West asked Muslim organizations in their countries to distance themselves from Islam as preached by these nineteen terrorists. This plea was met with indignation from Muslims who thought it was inappropriate to hold them responsible for the criminal conduct of nineteen young men. Yet the fact that the people who committed the attacks on September 11 were Muslims, and the fact that before this date Muslims in many parts of the world were already harboring feelings of immense resentment toward the United States in particular, have urged me to investigate whether the roots of evil can be traced to the faith I grew up with: was the aggression, the hatred inherent in Islam itself?

My parents brought me up to be a Muslim—a good Muslim. Islam dominated the lives of our family and relations down to the smallest detail. It was our ideology, our political conviction, our moral standard, our law, and our identity. We were first and foremost Muslim and only then Somali. Muslims, as we were taught the meaning of the name, are people who submit themselves to Allah's will, which is found in the Koran and the Hadith, a collection of sayings ascribed to the Prophet Muhammad. I was taught that Islam sets us apart from the rest of the world, the world of non-Muslims. We Muslims are chosen by God. They, the others, the *kaffirs*, the unbelievers, are antisocial, impure, barbaric, not circumcised, immoral, unscrupulous, and above all, obscene; they have no respect for women; their girls and women are whores; many of the men are homosexual; men and women have sex without being married. The unfaithful are cursed, and God will punish them most atrociously in the hereafter.

When my sister and I were small, we would occasionally make remarks about nice people who were not Muslim, but my mother and grandmother would always say, "No, they are not good people. They know about the Koran and the Prophet and Allah, and yet they haven't come to see that the only thing a person can be is Muslim. They are blind. If they were such nice and good people, they would have become Muslims and then Allah would protect them against evil. But it is up to them. If they become Muslims, they will go to paradise."

There are also Christians and Jews who raise their children in the belief that they are God's chosen people, but among Muslims the feeling that God has granted them special salvation goes further.

About twelve years ago, at age twenty-two, I arrived in Western Europe, on the run from an arranged marriage. I soon learned that God and His truth had been humanized here. For Muslims life on earth is merely a transitory stage before the hereafter; but here people are also allowed to invest in their lives as mortals. What is more, hell seems no longer to exist, and God is a god of love rather than a cruel ruler who metes out punishments. I began to take a more critical look at my faith and discovered three important elements of Islam that had not particularly struck me before.

The first of these is that a Muslim's relationship with his God is one of fear. A Muslim's conception of God is absolute. Our God demands total submission. He rewards you if you follow His rules meticulously. He punishes you cruelly if you break His rules, both on earth, with illness and natural disasters, and in the hereafter, with hellfire.

The second element is that Islam knows only one moral source: the Prophet Muhammad. Muhammad is infallible. You would almost believe he is himself a god, but the Koran says explicitly that Muhammad is a human being; he is a supreme human being, though, the most perfect human being. We must live our lives according to his example. What is written in the Koran is what God said as it was heard by Muhammad. The thousands of *hadiths*—accounts of what Muhammad said and did, and the advice he gave, which survives in weighty books—tell us exactly how a Muslim was supposed to live in the seventh century. Devout Muslims consult these works daily to answer questions about life in the twenty-first century.

The third element is that Islam is strongly dominated by a sexual morality derived from tribal Arab values dating from the time the Prophet received his instructions from Allah, a culture in which women were the property of their fathers, brothers, uncles, grandfathers, or guardians. The essence of a woman is reduced to her hymen. Her veil functions as a constant reminder to the outside world of this stifling morality that makes Muslim men the owners of women and obliges them to prevent their mothers, sisters, aunts, sisters-in-law, cousins, nieces, and wives from having sexual contact. And we are not just talking about cohabitation. It is an offense if a woman glances in the direction of a man, brushes past his arm, or shakes his hand. A man's reputation and honor depend entirely on the respectable, obedient behavior of the female members of his family.

These three elements explain largely why Muslim nations are lagging behind the West and, more recently, also lagging behind Asia. In order to break through the mental bars of this trinity, behind which the majority of Muslims are restrained, we must begin with a critical self-examination. But any Muslim who asks critical questions about Islam is immediately branded a "deserter." A Muslim who advocates the exploration of sources for morality, in addition to those of the Prophet Muhammad, will be threatened with death, and a woman who withdraws from the virgins' cage is branded a whore.

Through my personal experiences, through reading a great deal and speaking to others, I have come to realize that the existence of Allah, of angels, demons, and a life after death, is at the very least disputable. If Allah exists at all, we must not regard His word as absolute, but challenge it. I once wrote about my doubts regarding my faith in the hope of starting a discussion. I was immediately confronted by zealous Muslims, men and women who wanted to have me excommunicated. They even went so far as to say that I deserved to die because I had dared to call into question the absolute truth of Allah's word. They took me to court to prevent me from criticizing the faith I had been born into, from asking questions about the regulations and gods that Allah's messenger has imposed upon us. An Islamic fundamentalist murdered Theo van Gogh, the Dutch filmmaker who helped me make *Submission: Part I,* a film about the relationship between the individual and God, *in particular about the individual woman* and God. And he threatened to kill me, too, a threat that others have also pledged to fulfill.

Like other thinking people, I like to tap into sources of wisdom, morality, and imagination other than religious texts—other books besides the Koran and accounts of the Prophet—and I would like other Muslims to tap into them, too. Just because Spinoza, Voltaire, John Stuart Mill, Kant, or Bertrand Russell are not Islamic and have no Islamic counterparts does not mean that Muslims should steer clear of these and other Western philosophers. Yet, at present, reading works by Western thinkers is regarded as disrespectful to the Prophet and Allah's message. This is a serious misconception. Why should it not be permitted to abide by all the good things Muhammad has urged us to do (such as his advice to be charitable toward the poor and orphans), while at the same time adding to our lives and outlook the ideas of other moral philosophers? After all, the fact that the Wright brothers were not Islamic has not stopped Muslims from traveling by air. By adopting the technical inventions of the West without its courage to think independently, we perpetuate the mental stagnation in Islamic culture, passing it on from one generation to the next.

The most important explanation for the mental and material backlog we Muslims find ourselves in should probably be sought in the sexual morality that we are force-fed from birth (see chapter 3, "The Virgins' Cage"). I would like to invite all people like me who had an Islamic upbringing to compare and contrast J. S. Mill's essay "On the Subjection of Women" (1869) with what the Prophet Muhammad has to say on the subject of women. Both were undeniably interested in the role of women, but there is a vast difference between Muhammad and Mill. For instance, Mill considered his beloved wife an intellectual equal; Muhammad was a polygamist and wrote that men have authority over women because God made one superior to the other. Mill, a model of calm reason in the face of contentious issues, argued that if freedom is good for men, it is good for women, a position that today most of the modern world considers unassailable.

Yet any investigation into the Islamic trinity by a Muslim is thought to be an act of complete betrayal of the religion and the Prophet. It is extremely painful for a believer to try to question. And it is extremely painful for a believer to hear that other Muslims are questioning the Islamic trinity. Muslim's strong emotions and condemnations of people who do question the trinity impress outsiders, myself included, especially when they are expressed on a massive scale by entire communities and even nations, as has happened in Egypt, Iran, and Indonesia.

Think, for instance, of the murder of Theo van Gogh on the streets of Amsterdam, a Western city in a Western democracy, for exercising his free-speech rights to look critically at Islam in *Submission: Part I,* the film he and I made. While you may have heard of the death threats that have been made also against me for this film, you may not know that when I initially spoke on the immoral practices of the Prophet Muhammad, more than one hundred fifty complaints were made against me to the police and the government. Four ambassadors visited my party leaders—ambassadors from Saudi Arabia, Sudan, Pakistan, Malaysia. They carried a letter attached to which was a list of twenty-one countries belonging to the Islamic Conference—including Turkey—that supported the letter. The main complaint in their letter was that I had insulted the Prophet and had deeply hurt the feelings of more than 1 billion Muslims. Death threats followed against me and also against the leader of my party when he refused to take seriously this complaint and evict me from Parliament.

Think also of the reaction to the Miss World beauty pageant in Nigeria in 2002. Religious extremists protested the holding of the contest and became violently inflamed when a Christian journalist in an independent newspaper suggested, in reply to the scolding question, What would the Prophet Muhammad make of this improper display of women's beauty and bodies?, that the Prophet may have chosen a new wife from the contestants had he been alive today. This was felt to be a grave insult to the Prophet. During the subsequent protests, the office of the newspaper was burned down; two hundred people were killed and at least five hundred were injured.

Think also of the aftermath of *Newsweek*'s story in May 2005, of a 2002 FBI report made available to the journalist, that a soldier had flushed a Koran down a toilet at Guantánamo Bay, where Afghan and Pakistani soldiers suspected of being Taliban members are being held after capture in Afghanistan. Violent protests erupted in Pakistan and Afghanistan and lasted for several days; at least sixteen people were killed.

Think also of the situation that began in Denmark when the author of a biography of Muhammad wanted a drawing on his book jacket that represented the Prophet. All the artists he approached said, No, we can't do it; we fear Muslim reprisals and would fear for our lives. Hearing of the author's challenge, the daily newspaper *Jyllands-Posten* asked cartoonists to depict the Prophet as a test of whether freedom of expression had been limited in Denmark as a result of Islamic terrorists. Twelve cartoonists agreed, and the newspaper published their images in September 2005. Muslim organizations immediately demanded an apology, which the editor-in-chief refused to make, saying that a democracy makes use of all means of expression, including satire, and the images were not intended to insult the Prophet or Muslims. Nonetheless, 3,000 of the 187,000 Muslims living in Denmark protested the paper, which had to post guards as a result of death threats. Eleven foreign ambassadors visited the paper to complain. Months later, in January 2006, Muslim countries began to boycott Danish products. The Danish economy lost some 90 million euros in about a week; companies were forced to lay off hundreds of employees. In February, newspapers in other European countries published the images in support of Denmark and freedom of the press. Islamic extremists attacked and burned the Danish embassy in Beirut; one person was killed. Other European embassies in Islamic countries were attacked. A Christian priest was killed by a Turkish man screaming "God is great." As protests were fomented around the world, violence increased and the death toll mounted. Some moderate Muslims who called for restraint in Islamic countries were silenced by their governments, even jailed. Yet European governments are seriously considering limiting the freedom of the press to discuss Islam; some newspaper editors were fired for printing the cartoons. The tragedy for many Muslims is that their inability to criticize the dogma of religion in their own countries will be continued in Europe.

I am amazed that Muslims are not more offended by the invocation of Allah and "God is great" for murder than by cartoons. Why do Muslims not fly into flights of rage when people who go to help Iraqis are kidnapped, tortured, and beheaded in the name of Islam?

Political cartoons that point up problems with an extremist religion are used to manipulate people into violence instead of reflection and debate. Freedom of expression for Muslims is a one-way street; Muslims can criticize the West, but the West cannot criticize the practices of Islam.

I understand that a Muslim may feel a duty to scold anyone who attempts to call into question the absoluteness of God's word or someone who regards other sources of morality as equal, or superior even, to the Prophet Muhammad's. History shows that for many people to make a mental transition of this magnitude and question their beliefs is always a very slow process, and one that generates resistance and causes bloodshed. In this context I can place the murder of Theo van Gogh, the death threats and legal steps against me, and the intense rejection and condemnation of me as an individual, a heretic, and a blasphemer. Remember that the Protestant Reformation took many years of protest (the source of its name) as well as bloodshed and widespread unrest to establish itself firmly. A quick look at Islamic history shows us that critical voices from within Islam have almost all been either killed or exiled. I find myself in good company: Salman Rushdie, Irshad Manji, Taslima Nasreen, Muhammad Abu Zaid—they all have been threatened by fellow believers and are now being guarded by non-Muslims.

Nonetheless we who were brought up with Islam must summon the courage to break through this wall of emotional resistance or to climb over it, until eventually the number of critics grows large enough to counterbalance the entrenched opposition effectively. In order to achieve this we will need the help of the liberal West, whose interests are greatly served by a reform of Islam. But above all, we Muslims must help each other.

I am feeling optimistic about that reform. I base my optimism on positive signs, like the local elections in Saudi Arabia (although women were excluded from these elections, at least the elections were held); the successful elections in Iraq and Afghanistan (where a secular government has taken over after the Taliban); the demonstrations against the terror of the Islamic Party by journalists and academics in Morocco; and the promising agreements between Sharon and Abbas about the future of Israel and Palestine. Abbas is more reasonable than the late Arafat and seems to act in the interest of the Palestinians, and Israel's giving back the land to the Palestinians for self-rule is good progress, although the election in which Hamas became the ruling party is a setback. Another indication of progress is Pakistan's acceptance of Israeli aid to the victims of the terrible October 8, 2005, earthquake. Of course, I realize that these are quite recent developments.

I am optimistic, and I normally would have looked to the West for help in reforming Islam, from secular liberals, Westerners who are traditionally opposed to the enforcement of religious beliefs and customs. In certain countries, "left-wing," secular liberals have stimulated my critical thinking and that of other Muslims. But these same liberals in Western politics have the strange habit of blaming themselves for the ills of the world, while seeing the rest of the world as victims. To them, victims are to be pitied, and they lump together all pitiable and suppressed people, such as Muslims, and consider them good people who should be cherished and supported so that they can overcome their disadvantages. The adherents to the gospel of multiculturalism refuse to criticize people whom they see as victims. Some Western critics disapprove of United States policies and attitudes but do not criticize the Islamic world, just as, in the first part of the twentieth century, Western socialist apologists did not dare criticize the Soviet labor camps. Along the same lines, some Western intellectuals criticize Israel, but they will not criticize Palestine because Israel belongs to the West, which they consider fair game, but they feel sorry for the Palestinians, and for the Islamic world in general, which is not as powerful as the West. They are critical of the native white majority in Western countries but not of Islamic minorities. Criticism of the Islamic world, of Palestinians, and of Islamic minorities is regarded as Islamophobia and xenophobia.

I cannot emphasize enough how wrongheaded this is. Withholding criticism and ignoring differences are racism in its purest form. Yet these cultural experts fail to notice that, through their anxious avoidance of criticizing non-Western countries, they trap the people who represent these cultures in a state of backwardness. The experts may have the best of intentions, but as we all know, the road to hell is paved with good intentions.

My own criticism of Islamic religion and culture is felt by some to be "harsh," "offensive," and "hurtful." But the attitude of the cultural experts is, in fact, harsher, and more offensive and hurtful. They feel superior and do not regard Muslims as equal discussion partners, but as the "others" who should be shielded. And they think that criticism of Islam should be avoided because they are afraid that Muslims can only respond to criticism with anger and violence. These cultural experts are badly letting down us Muslims who have obeyed the call to show our sense of public responsibility and are speaking out.

I have taken an enormous risk by answering the call for self-reflection and by joining in the public debate that has been taking place in the West since 9/11. And what do the cultural experts say? "You should have said it in a different way." But since Theo van Gogh's death, I have been convinced more than ever that I must say it in *my* way only and have *my* criticism.

ONE

Stand Up for Your Rights!

Women in Islam

I was born in Somalia in 1969 and raised in an Islamic family. My father, Hirsi Magan, is a well-known opposition leader who challenged the dictatorship of Mohamed Siad Barre. Probably in 1975 or 1976, he was forced to flee Somalia, and our family followed him. Via Saudi Arabia and Ethiopia, we reached Kenya.

At age twenty-two, as a Muslim young woman, I was given in marriage to a distant cousin, a nephew of my father's. Had we been married, I would have lived out my days in isolation as a housewife and mother. But I refused to attend the wedding ceremony, which was to be held in Canada, and shortly afterward I escaped to the Netherlands. There, I applied for and was granted asylum, learned Dutch, worked as an interpreter in a number of places—including abortion clinics and women's refuge centers—and took a degree in political science.

That was ten years ago. In the Netherlands, I am able to study and work. I can also voice my opinion here. Through newspapers, magazines, television, and radio, I have criticized Islam and the Islamic community. My comments stir up strong feelings. The attention I strove to give to the plight of Muslim women in the Netherlands and Western Europe led to my becoming a parliamentary representative, at first for the Labor Party and, after October 2002, for the Liberal Party. My change of parties also stirred up strong feelings. In the United States, it would have been analogous to switching from the Democratic Party to the Republican. Some of my former party felt betrayed by my switch, but I viewed it as a practical matter. I believe I have more support in the Liberal Party for my mission to help Muslim women.

I am often asked why I, in particular, am so critical of Islam and of the position of women within Islam. I am accused of discrediting that religion through my opinions and comments. Allegedly, I portray *all* Muslim men as "stupid and violent louts who repress their women." I am further blamed for playing into the hands of populists and racists, who will misuse my opinions to repress Muslims. Yet I continue to feel compelled to speak out against the way women are treated within the Muslim community. There are four reasons that I do this.

———•———

I hope to be able to make a contribution to ending the degrading treatment of Muslim women and girls by using my knowledge and experience of the Muslim faith. I am a passionate believer in universal human rights. As a member of the board of directors of Amnesty International, I am distressed that the vast majority of Muslim women are still enchained by the doctrine of virginity, which requires that women enter marriage as green as grass: experience of love and sexuality before marriage is an absolute taboo. This taboo does not apply to men. Furthermore, men and women do not have equal rights or opportunities in any way within their specific Muslim culture. Many women simply lack all opportunity to organize their lives independently or as they see fit.

I do not despise Islam. I am thoroughly conscious of the noble values that the religion promotes, such as charity, hospitality, and compassion for the weak and poor. But for women, the situation is very different. In the name of Islam, women are subjected to cruel and horrible practices, including female genital mutilation and disownment, the latter a common practice in which women are cut off from their families both emotionally and financially for any perceived misbehavior.

Obviously, far from all Muslim men are disrespectful or violent toward women. I know countless wonderful Muslim men who treat their mothers, sisters, and spouses decently. Moreover, men are every bit as much victims of the culture of virginity as women, albeit indirectly. As a result of this repressive culture, boys and men are not raised by healthy, balanced, and well-educated mothers. This in turn puts men themselves at a disadvantage when pursuing education, employment, and social development.

Because of the disproportionately strong emphasis on "manliness" in the Muslim upbringing and because of the physical and mental separation of the sexes, men hardly have the opportunity to develop the communication skills necessary for living harmoniously within a family. It is therefore not surprising that many Muslim women in the Netherlands complain that their husbands seldom talk to them. Muslim marriages, prearranged by the family when the daughter is very young, give men heavy responsibilities that are not of their own choosing—for girls they scarcely know.

These expectations often breed a lack of self-understanding and a lack of understanding of women. Feelings of anger and powerlessness are common among men. Moreover, if, as a man, you are raised with the idea that it is all right to hit a woman, then the step to using violence is only a small one. At the present time, women's shelters in the Netherlands have a large influx of Muslim women seeking refuge from violent husbands. Separate shelters for Muslim girls escaping their parental homes have also been set up.

Ironically, the repression of women is maintained to a large extent by other women. Here is what Fatma Katirci, a Turkish *imama* (the female worshiper who leads the prayers of women who pray together—on the occasions when they can) in Amsterdam, says about the verse in the Koran that gives men the right to beat their wives: "The conflict cannot be about what will be on the table that night. It has to be about a serious issue, like a question of honor, such as infidelity. If a woman harms the family's reputation through her behavior . . . You see, some women learn from just a good talk; others only think better of their actions if the beds are separated, and some are truly neurotic. For the latter, a little slap can be the very last resort to get them to see the error of their ways. Don't misunderstand me: I'm against it. Beating is degrading, but if there's really no alternative, then it has to happen."

This statement reveals that even educated women often have difficulty relinquishing ideas that have been instilled in them since childhood. In the traditionally oriented Muslim communities, it is often the mothers who keep their daughters under their thumbs and the mothers-in-law who make the lives of their daughters-in-law unbearable. Cousins and aunts gossip endlessly about one another and about others. The effect of this social control is that Muslim women maintain their own repression.

The second reason for my critical stance is the danger that, without the emancipation of Muslim women, the socially disadvantageous position of Muslims will persist in Western countries as well as the entire world. I see a direct link between the poor situation of Muslim women, on the one hand, and the lagging behind of Muslims in education and the job market, their high rate of juvenile delinquency, and their heavy reliance on social services on the other. In reality, the upbringing of Muslim girls denies them personal independence and their own sense of responsibility, values that are essential for getting ahead in a Western country.

It is a dangerous development that the age at which girls can be married off in a country like the Netherlands, and in every Western country with a major Muslim minority, has dropped in the past few years. To marry someone off is to make a girl or young woman available to a man unknown to her who is then allowed to use her sexually. The younger the bride, the greater the chance she will be a virgin. In essence, what is involved here is an arranged rape approved of by her entire family. Marrying off usually implies the girl is not able or allowed to complete her education. Tragically, countless Muslim girls still have to comply with this practice.

Girls who are not successful in preserving their virginity or who are afraid (despite the fact that they have never had sex) that they won't bleed on their wedding night resort to medical interventions that restore their hymens. Approximately ten to fifteen of these operations are performed in Dutch hospitals every month. As a result of the taboo on sex—and thus on sex education—Muslim girls and women end up with undesired pregnancies or infected with sexually transmitted diseases. The increase in abortions is directly related to the influx of Moroccan and Turkish women.

The third reason I am determined to make my voice heard is that Muslim women are scarcely listened to, and they need a woman to speak out on their behalf. Their official spokespersons are nearly all men. Given the widespread suffering of Muslim women, there are too few social organizations and political parties actively devoted to improving their lot. Spokesmen of Muslim organizations and immigrant politicians with Muslim backgrounds, along with other advocates of "group rights," excel in denying, trivializing, or avoiding the enormous problems of Muslim girls and women in the West.

In a June 2002 interview, the member of parliament for the Socialist Party, Khadija Arib, said the following about the position of Muslim women: "People seem to think that immigrant women want to sit home alone all day, but this happens mostly because there is nowhere for them to go." At the opening in spring of a mother-and-child daycare center in an Amsterdam suburb, she proposed establishing a special facility where women could attend activities all day long. In doing so, she denies the essence of the problem. In a large segment of the Muslim community, the notion still exists that women should not have any freedom of movement or work outside the home. Muslim women will benefit more from harsh criticism of this idea than from the creation of special women's activity centers.

——•——

My final motive is my firm belief that the emphasis on a Muslim identity with corresponding "group rights" is detrimental to Muslim women. In 1999, Susan Moller Okin, a professor of political science and a feminist, launched a discussion in the United States between the advocates of multiculturalism, who favor the advancement and preservation of Islamic (or other) group cultures, and the opponents of multiculturalism, including Okin herself. In her view, the fact that many Western governments pursue a policy geared to the preservation of group cultures is in conflict with their constitutions which, after all, set down the principles of individual freedom and the equality of men and women. Among other criticisms, she points out that multiculturalists take no heed of the private lives of the cultures they are defending. And it is precisely in private life that differences in power and the repression of women manifest themselves most clearly.

——•——

In the final analysis, Muslim women in the West will benefit more from the dominant Western culture that is adhered to by the majority of the population and that offers them good opportunities to shape their lives according to their own insights. I am the living proof of this. This is also why I feel responsible for preserving and protecting the democratic system to which I personally owe so much. In principle, all Dutch Muslims have the same human rights, but owing to outdated religious opinions, they are scarcely capable of implementing these rights. It is mostly women who are affected, and this is what I find distressing.

People who *have* been successful in Western societies, who share the faith of the repressed women (their numbers, incidentally, are not very large), should stand up more for their sisters and brothers.

I would like to encourage women such as Naima El Bezaz, who writes openheartedly about women and sexuality, to rise above the religious barrier to question the source of the culture of virginity (Koran, Hadith, a collection of the Prophet's sayings, traditions, and the resulting practices) rather than to continue to take for granted established tradition. This would be to their own advantage *and* to that of those who share their fate but who have thus far had fewer opportunities to develop themselves. I call to account members of parliament such as Khadija Arib, Nebahat Albayrak, Naima Azough, and Fatima Elatik. The logic of establishing priorities demands that first things be put first. Less serious issues like the "image of Islam" must yield as a consequence. Is it not absurd to imagine that Allah, in all His greatness, would be worried about His image?

I invite the advocates of the multicultural society to acquaint themselves with the suffering of the women who, in the name of religion, are enslaved in the home. Do you have to be mistreated, raped, locked up, and repressed yourself in order to put yourself in someone else's position? Is it not hypocritical to trivialize or tolerate those practices, when you yourself are free and benefit from mankind's progress?

A multicultural society is not a goal in itself. We in the West need to make a concerted effort to counter Islamic education and all those other Islamic institutions that lead to self-segregation and thus contribute to the continuation of a hopeless tyranny over women and children.

TWO

Why Can't We Take a Critical Look at Ourselves?

It has been pointed out ad nauseam that a single Islam does not exist. There are as many Islams as there are Muslims. One Muslim considers Islam to be an identity; another, a culture; a third, purely a religion. For yet another, Islam represents everything at once: identity, culture, religion, as well as a political and social guide. But despite these discrepancies, all Muslims share the conviction that the fundamental principles of Islam cannot be criticized, revised, or in any way contradicted. The sources of Islam are the Koran and the sayings and deeds of the prophet (the Sunnah), and every Muslim has the duty to emulate these words and deeds as closely as possible in his morals and daily life. In this context I wish to pose the question, Should we fear Islam? I ask that we *do* question the fundamental principles.

Following the horrendous attacks of September 11, it became known that the name of the suspected chief perpetrator was Mohammed Atta. The young man left behind a note in which he declared that he committed his act of terror for Allah, and for the reward awaiting him in paradise. The letter also included the text of a prayer in which he asks Allah to give him strength and to stand by him and his act.

A short time later, Mohammed Atta's father appeared on television. When confronted with his son's act, Father Atta was enraged and, at the same time, sad. He appeared confused; he couldn't and didn't want to believe that his son was guilty of the mass murder on September 11. His son was, he said, a thoughtful, peace-loving boy. Moreover, he had no reason whatsoever to take part in such an act of terrorism. He was, after all, highly educated by Egyptian standards. His German professor confirmed that Mohammed Atta was a very promising architect. In short, Mohammed had all the qualities of a successful young man with a wonderful future ahead of him; his father was extremely proud. No, no, Father Atta cried, my son has nothing to do with it: the Jews, the CIA, everybody and everything is guilty, but not my son. Ill-intentioned people want to give my son and me a bad name and tarnish our honor.

At the same time, during those early days after September 11, Muslims writers, theologians, imams, as well as ordinary Muslim men and women, were confronted with the same questions: How could nineteen committed Muslims carry out such a despicable act in the name of their religion? Why does Bin Laden call on all Muslims to participate in a war against nonbelievers in the name of their religion? Why do Indonesian, Pakistani, and even British Muslims want to comply with Bin Laden's call and sacrifice their lives in the name of their religion?

The reactions of these Muslims were similar to that of Father Atta: both shock and indignation at the idea that Islam was being linked to terrorism. No, they cried emphatically and in unison: the perpetrators were not Muslims; some boys might drink and visit prostitutes, but these are non-Islamic habits that they picked up from the decadent West; they cited verses from the Koran completely out of context. No, Bin Laden is not a Muslim. No, all those shrieking young men celebrating 9/11 in the streets of cities in Muslim countries have misunderstood Islam: Islam is a peace-loving, tolerant, charitable religion. Whoever loves Allah and honors the bearer of His tidings will never want to cause trouble for other believers and nonbelievers, let alone kill them or participate in terrorist activities.

But if this is true, how then are we to explain the facts? What am I, as a Muslim, to think when I read that:

- Muslims were responsible for eleven, and possibly twelve, of the sixteen major international terrorist acts committed between 1983 and 2000;

- Five of the seven states that support terrorists, and as such appear on the U.S. State Department's list, are Muslim countries, and the majority of foreign organizations on that same list are Muslim organizations;

- Muslims were involved in two-thirds of the thirty-two armed conflicts in the year 2000, while only one-fifth of the world population is Muslim, according to the London-based International Institute of Strategic Studies.

If nothing is wrong with Islam, why then are so many Muslims on the run? Of the top ten countries from which people have emigrated to the Netherlands, nine are primarily Muslim. Why do we Muslims move to the West, while at the same time condemning it? What does the West have that we don't? Why is the position of women in Muslim countries so abominable? If we Muslims are so tolerant and peaceful, why is there so much ethnic, religious, political, and cultural strife and violence in Muslim countries? Why can't or won't we acknowledge the seriousness of the situation in which we find ourselves? Why are we Muslims so full of feelings of anger and uneasiness, and why do we carry so much hostility and hate within us both toward ourselves and toward others? Why are we incapable of criticizing ourselves from within?

If I had to characterize Islam, I would say that it has become like Father Atta: incensed, traumatized, shattered, and living in an illusion. Just as Atta fathered his son Mohammed, so Islam has fathered a branch that we alternately call fundamentalism or political Islam. Just as the father didn't see that his son had a darker side, so too, for a long time, we Muslims have refused to acknowledge that a once peaceful, powerful, and robust religion carried within it elements of fanaticism and violence. We wanted, and still want, a Muslim solution for everything. We have always left the course of our lives, the organization of our society, our economic policy, the education of our children, and the relationship between men and women in the hands of God. *Insha'allah* (if God [Allah] wills it) is the most common expression among Muslims.

We Muslims have completely lost sight of the balance between religion and reason. Poverty, violence, political instability, economic malaise, and human suffering are the result. Just as Father Atta is proud of his son, so we Muslims are proud of our Islam; we are unwilling and unable to believe that Allah no longer has the answers to all our questions, or if He does have them, He doesn't want to share them with us.

Yet there are a number of Muslims who do have doubts and who have already cautiously embarked on a process of self-examination and a quest for a way out of the labyrinth. They are a small minority and they still have to overcome both their own suffering and the fundamentalists' antagonism. But that is not all. They also have to fight the reactionary forces that have become so adept at using the constitutional freedoms of well-functioning democracies like the Netherlands to maintain the illusion in which the Muslim masses find themselves.

We can rephrase the question Should we fear Islam? to Should we fear Father Atta? How well founded is the fear we feel, and what do we do with that fear? It is human to fear the dangerous sides of a religion such as extremism and fanaticism, but it is also human to understand the pain of Muslims and to want to help them.

The reactionary regimes in the Middle East have been successful in convincing the United States that the only evil to be fought is the terrorism stemming from Islamic fundamentalism. The United

States fails to see that it is precisely these regimes and the clergy who keep them in power that are the secondary causes of fanaticism, or *Wahhabism*, as Saudi Arabia calls it. Given that the fundamentalists are the only opposition to the reactionary regimes, the policy of the United States will have the wrong effect. The "enemy" concept of fanatics like Bin Laden is reinforced by the actions of the United States. This is the bitter reality: the Muslim population is using Islam as a political tool by which to dispose of the repressive regimes, but the promises made by Muslim fundamentalists to the people offer no prospects of success whatsoever. This is why it is absolutely essential that Muslims begin to be critical of their religion and to review it from the inside, with help from the outside.

The West needs to help Muslims help themselves, and not support them in their illusion by avoiding the underlying questions. Despite the compassion and understanding one may feel for personal suffering, one cannot lose sight of the fact that this personal suffering is the inevitable result of the form Islam takes at home, at school, in everyday life, and in the media. Many Muslims lack the necessary willingness and courage to address this crucial issue. There is an essential difference between Father Atta's situation and that of Islam. Father Atta's son is dead; he can allow himself time to grapple with his trauma slowly. Unfortunately, Islam—we Muslims—do not have that luxury of time.

So what must happen? The primary task of both Muslims and non-Muslims is to face the malicious extremism manifest in the attacks of September 11. Do not underestimate it. Fear of that kind of Islam is valid. Fanaticism in Islam is a reality, and its following is growing steadily. Westerners and Muslims should stand together in their shared rejection of fanaticism, instead of blaming each other and cultivating mutual distrust. That solves nothing, and the fanatics may benefit from it.

The second task, for Muslims themselves, is that of enlightenment. We Muslims must realize the importance and urgency of restoring the balance between religion and reason, and work exceedingly hard at achieving it. Religion offers no appropriate solution for the clamorous situation in which Muslims find themselves worldwide. We must structurally drive religion back to the places where it belongs: in the mosque and in the home. We Muslims are inclined to view universal values, such as freedom of the individual and the equality of men and women, as exclusively Western values. This is wrong. We need to apply these values to ourselves and start creating political and legal institutions that can protect and promote those values. We also need to begin to engage in rational and scientific analysis. It is true that these values and methods were born out of Western tradition, but that does not mean they are any less pertinent for people in other parts of the world. If they were not, people would not be fleeing to the West in such large numbers. To achieve the aforementioned goals requires a fundamental shift in Muslim mentality. This change can only begin by subjecting the sources of Islam to thorough critical examination.

The third task is primarily one that pertains to Western non-Muslims who have already benefited for a long time from the fruits of the Enlightenment. Intellectuals and authorities must assist us in our pursuit of reason. This undertaking holds within it a dilemma: how can the West preserve an open, tolerant society based on the notion of rights and combat rightist extremism and religious intolerance, while helping Muslims with their process of enlightenment? Thus far, politicians and policy makers, as well as intellectuals, have been afraid to confront Muslims about the opinions, customs, and practices arising from their religion that severely damage Muslims themselves and society. At present, the reactionary forces within Islam continue to gain power. Just as the regimes in the Middle East are manipulating the United States in order to consolidate their own power, so too are countless Muslim organizations in the Netherlands managing to maintain their conservative opinions and practices, in particular regarding the position of women in their culture. The Dutch government is among those who pay heed to these reactionary forces in misguided ways. For example, the mayor of

Amsterdam, Job Cohen, called on secular people to respect the unifying power of religion. As is typical of so much muzz-headed, empty political rhetoric, it is unclear what he was really asking, but he apparently believed that Islam is primarily a religious practice that provides comfort to immigrant followers by drawing them together in a community. He seemed to be making an appeal to the Dutch people to adopt an unreflective, unexamined tolerance of Islamic communities and their activities. With this "appeal," however, he blatantly ignored the desperate situation of Muslim women in his own city. And he seemed to believe—mistakenly—that this "benevolent" sentiment and attitude would help the integration of Muslims into Dutch society.

It will not. It does exactly the opposite: it makes a virtual institution of Muslim self-segregation and isolation. The mayor's misguided, benighted complicity with the Islamists' agenda has earned him the honorary title of "sheikh" among reactionaries. Similarly, in another example of fuzzy thinking, Roger van Boxtel, the Dutch Minister for Urban Policy and Integration of Ethnic Minorities, stubbornly persists in defending Islamic education, which is precisely what perpetuates the poverty and alienation of Muslim peoples. For his knee-jerk support, van Boxtel earned the title of "mullah" among reactionaries.

Whatever the mayor's point in his supposed humanistic appeal, he and other Westerners have to understand that we Muslims have religion inculcated in us from birth, and that is one of the very reasons for our falling behind the West in technology, finance, health, and culture. Sheikh Cohen and Mullah van Boxtel should realize that we Muslims are already imbued with faith and superstition. What we need are schools of philosophy and the liberation of our women. Has Sheikh Cohen ever visited a women's refuge center in his city? If he had, he could not have failed to see some of the chiefly hidden yet omnipresent and undeniable suffering of Muslim women. Neither the Islam and Citizenship Society nor the Muslim community says anything about their women's suffering, and every one of the 753 subsidized Muslim organizations in the Netherlands also remains silent about it. Only aid organizations such as the Regional Institute for Mental Welfare, the Child Welfare Council, and the Central Registration for Child Abuse recognize the suffering. Muslims report there in large numbers. But these and other aid organizations are also unable to speak out because of their duty to respect confidentiality.

There is a strict taboo in Muslim families on talking about birth control, abortion, and sexual violence. That taboo is a direct result of our religion. A girl who is pregnant keeps quiet about it at home. The unifying power of her religion works only negatively, as pure repression. The result is not unity or solidarity, but inner conflict and terrible loneliness. The only way out is the abortion clinic, where Islamic girls are frequently helped, a suffering they again bear in silence. Sixty percent of all abortions in the Netherlands involve immigrant women, many of whom have an Islamic background.

So it is clear that the fear of Islam is already present in the Netherlands. Politicians and policy makers in that country are already too afraid to confront us Muslims with our illusions. And thus the fear of offending leads to the perpetuation of injustice and human suffering.

THREE

The Virgins' Cage

Arab culture has spread to non-Arab societies by way of Islam, but is in many ways far behind that of the West. The three main shortcomings are insufficient individual freedom, inadequate knowledge, and a lack of women's rights. These problems may also be seen in non-Arab countries that have embraced Islam and have begun to follow the Koran and the Hadith as political and economic guides for how a community should be organized. In countries such as Pakistan and Iran, and to a lesser extent in parts of Indonesia, Malaysia, Nigeria, and Tanzania, after the introduction of Islam, a significant regression occurred in individual freedom, the acquisition of scientific knowledge, and the rights of women.

There are prospects for improvement, but progress is slow. The United Nations reports on *Arab Human Development,* prepared by Arab scholars, are first steps in the right direction, and they identified the core of these problems. The Arab world's current wealth comes exclusively from the oil that is extracted by Western corporations. Its economic growth is the lowest in the world, with exception of sub-Saharan Africa; illiteracy is widespread and persistent. Only about 330 foreign books are translated per year in the entire Arab world (compared to 5,000 in the Netherlands alone and close to 400 in the United States). The situation for human rights is equally dire. Arab authorities use force against their own people, and population groups employ violence against each other.

People are oppressed, and the position of women is, in my view, nowhere as bad as it is in the Islamic world. United Nations reports state that women are virtually excluded from any public and political life, and that legislation with respect to marriage, divorce, inheritance, and adultery puts women at an extreme disadvantage.

The same disadvantaged state of affairs in the Islamic world is reflected to a lesser degree in the position of Muslim immigrants in Western Europe. Muslims who have immigrated to Western Europe have brought their convictions and traditions with them. It is striking that in the West, Muslim men are overrepresented in prisons and Muslim women are overrepresented in shelters for abused women and the social-assistance system. Many Muslims fare poorly in school and in the job market. They only rarely take advantage of the opportunities offered in education and employment, and they do not sufficiently benefit from the freedoms that were unavailable in their countries of origin.

What is blocking the progress of Muslims? Why can't they close the gap between themselves and the Western world? Why can't they participate in Western society the way other immigrants do?

According to some experts, Western imperialism and unfavorable climatic conditions are at the root of the lagging development of Muslims. Many Islamic states were created too suddenly and artificially and became dictatorships. The dictators having been installed and maintained by Western states, thereby retarding Muslim development. However, historian Bernard Lewis convincingly refutes this claim. He believes the delay in Muslim development arises out of Muslims' feelings of grievance against Westerners. For centuries, dating back to even before the Middle Ages, Muslims saw Westerners as stupid and backward, lacking in cleanliness, morals, and civilized conduct. The Moors, who conquered Spain and ruled there for seven hundred years before 1492, were responsible for introducing basic hygiene, for preserving the great Roman and Greek classics, for introducing modern agricultural practices such as irrigation, and for a great flowering of culture. Starting in the twelfth century, however, the Muslim mind-set became less tolerant, less inquisitive, more extremist in its views. At the same time, the Judeo-Christian West realized it needed to improve, and its people began learning, traveling, and exploring. As a result, the West caught up with Islamic culture and overtook it in a very short time.

An explanation from the Islamic point of view is provided by Sayyid Qutb and Hassan al-Banna, the founders of radical Islam. According to them, the *umma,* the community, can flourish only if its members keep to the letter of the Koran and the Hadith, the traditions of the Prophet Muhammad. They are of the view that Muslims have strayed from the path that the Prophet Muhammad outlined for them and have thereby brought their misery upon themselves. But actually, politics that follow Islam to the letter have failed dramatically. Islam does not possess a credible and workable political model, as the wavering regimes in Iran and Saudi Arabia illustrate. The Islamists are correct in stating that the huge majority of Muslims do not succeed in closely following all the commands and prohibitions of Allah. Nor should Muslims follow them, nor will they be able to follow them as long as these proscriptions are defined by fundamentalists.

The problems—aggression, economic and scientific stagnation, repression, epidemics, and social unrest—that confront most of the world's 1.2 billion Muslims spread over five continents cannot be explained by simply one or two factors. A complex combination of factors, sometimes regional, has evolved over time, one of which is the sexual morality of Islam, originally a tribal morality that has been elevated within Islam to the status of a dogma. This explanation appears too rarely in the existing literature. This premodern morality was sanctified in the Koran and then further developed in the traditions of the Prophet. For many Muslims this morality expresses itself through an obsession with virginity. This obsession with mastery over the sexuality of women is not limited to Islam, but is also evident in other religions (e.g., among Christians, Jews, and Hindus). Yet it has not hindered these other religious cultures' modern development as much as it has the Muslims'. The value attached to a woman's virginity is so great that it eclipses the human catastrophes and social costs that result from it.

Muslim girls are often told that "a girl with a ruptured hymen is like a used object." And an object that is once used becomes permanently worthless. A girl who has lost her "seal of being unused" won't find a marriage partner and is doomed to spend the rest of her days in her parents' home. Moreover, if defloration occurs outside wedlock, she has dishonored her family to the tenth degree of kinship. Other families will gossip about them. They will say that the family is known for its loose women who throw themselves away to "the first man who comes along." So the girl is punished by her family. Punishments range from name-calling to expulsion or confinement and may even extend to a shotgun wedding either to the man who is responsible for the defloration or to some "generous man" willing to cover the family's shame. These so-called generous men are often poor, feebleminded, old, impotent, or all of these. In the worst-case scenario, the girl will be murdered, often by her own family. The United Nations reports that five thousand girls are murdered annually for this reason in Islamic countries, including Jordan, so often cited as a "liberal" regime.

To avoid this cruel fate, Muslim families do everything possible to ensure that their daughters' hymens remain intact before marriage. The methods vary according to the country and specific circumstances in which people live and the means available to them. But everywhere the measures are aimed at girls, the possessors of the hymen, and not at the men who could break it.

Not long ago the spokesman for the Turkish Ministry of Justice, Professor Dogan Soyasian, stated that all men want to marry virgins, and that men who deny this are hypocrites. A raped woman is still advised to marry the man who raped her, the argument being that time heals all wounds. In time the woman will be able to love her rapist, and they may become very happy together. But if the woman has been raped by several men, a marriage like that will have a lower chance of success because her husband will see her as a dishonorable woman.

When it concerns their sexuality, men in Islamic culture are seen as irresponsible, unpredictable, scary beasts who immediately lose all self-control upon seeing a woman. This reminds me of an experience I had when I was still quite young. My grandmother had a billy goat. We were playing in front of the house, and in the evening, just before it got dark, all the goats in the neighborhood returned home in a long procession. It was a charming sight. But as soon as Grandma's billy goat saw the other goats, he galloped over to them and mounted the first goat he could get hold of. We children thought this was very cruel. When we asked Grandma what her goat was doing, she answered that it was none of her business: if the neighbours didn't want their goats to be mounted, they should lead them home along another path. Islam represents its own men as though they were like that billy goat; when Muslim men see an uncovered woman, they immediately leap on her. This becomes a self-fulfilling prophecy; a Muslim man has no reason to learn to control himself. He doesn't need to and he isn't taught to. Sexual morality is aimed exclusively at women, who are always blamed for any lapse.

From a very young age, girls are surrounded by an atmosphere of mistrust. They learn early that they are untrustworthy beings who constitute a danger for the clan. Something in them drives men crazy. To illustrate this attitude, let me tell you of an exchange I had with Achmed, a father I met at an Islamic school last year who told me that in the past he had been a nonpracticing Muslim. He drank, committed adultery, and paid virtually no attention to the pillars of Islam. A few years ago he had been converted, as he himself put it. He read the Koran and decided to raise his daughter in the Islamic way. I asked him why his daughter, a child of seven, had to wear the *hijab*, the headscarf. "I know Islam," I said to him. "The *hijab* isn't needed until a girl reaches puberty." "Yes," he said, "but she has to learn to wear it, so that later it will seem natural." He explained to me the rules of Islam concerning the *hijab* and said, "Here in the Netherlands women wear very little in the summer. That leads to accidents." Achmed had himself witnessed such an accident, he told me. Last summer he saw one truck collide with another. "The truck driver who caused the accident wasn't watching the road but was looking at the bare legs of a beautiful woman who was walking by."

For this reason girls have to cover themselves, make themselves invisible. And for this reason they feel constantly guilty and ashamed, because it is almost impossible to live a normal life *and* be invisible to men. Girls constantly think they're doing something wrong. Not only is their external freedom to choose where to go or where not to go inhibited, but so is their inner freedom. My aunt once put a piece of mutton out in the sun. It attracted columns of ants and swarms of flies. Auntie said, "Men are just like these ants and flies: when they see a woman they can't restrain their lust." I saw the fat melt in the sun as the ants and flies feasted on it. It left a dirty trace behind.

Girls' virginity is protected in various ways, one of which is house arrest, which can start at puberty. To secure their virginity, millions of Muslim women are sentenced to domestic work indoors and hours of endless boredom. Should it become absolutely necessary for a girl to go outside, she is allowed only if she keeps her head covered and dresses in a cloak that hides everything. This is to signal to men that she is sexually unavailable. To support this, the Koran is quoted "Stay quietly in your homes, and make not a dazzling display . . . And say to the believing women that they should lower their gaze and guard their modesty; that they should not display their beauty and ornaments except what [must ordinarily] appear thereof; that they should draw their veils over their bosoms and not display their beauty except to their husbands, their fathers, their husbands' fathers, their sons, their husbands' sons, their brothers, or their brothers' sons, or their sisters' sons, or their womenfolk, or those whom their right hands possess [their slaves], or male servants free of physical needs, or small children who have no sense of the shame of sex." "Oh, Prophet! Tell thy wives and daughters, and the believing women, that they should cast their outer garments over their persons [when abroad]: that is most convenient, that they may be known [as such] and not molested."

A second way of preserving virginity is to keep men and women who are not close family members in separate quarters indoors. This too amounts to house arrest. In Saudi Arabia, a bastion of Islam where the two holy houses of Allah (Mecca and Medina) are located, this division has been taken to extremes—other relatively oil-rich sheikhdoms, as well as Iran, Pakistan, Sudan, and Yemen, follow close behind.

By far the most extreme method of safeguarding virginity is female circumcision. The process involves the cutting away of the girl's clitoris, the outer and inner labia, as well as the scraping of the walls of her vagina with a sharp object—a fragment of glass, a razor blade, or a potato knife, and then the binding together of her legs, so that the walls of the vagina can grow together. This happens in more than thirty countries, including Egypt, Somalia, and Sudan. Although it is not prescribed in the Koran, for those Muslims who cannot do without the labor that girls perform outside the walls of their home, this originally tribal custom has practically become a religious duty, and is defended as such. Proponents point to the fact that the circumcision of women existed in the period before and during Muhammad's time, and that the Prophet Muhammad did not explicitly prohibit it. The so-called infibulation (literally "stitching up") offers a guarantee over women and is implemented under the watchful eyes of mothers, aunts, grandmothers, and other female guardians.

The distrust of women reaches its apex during the wedding night test: is the Muslim bride a virgin or not? Due to the gender apartheid that banishes women from public life, a Muslim man has no natural way to get to know a woman with whom he might fall in love. His family is therefore entrusted with the choice, as only they would know where to find a genuine virgin. Although the recently wedded pair often don't even know each other, they nevertheless must have intercourse on their wedding night. Even if the girl doesn't want to, and her body closes up in fear or disgust, she must. And even if her husband doesn't want to, either, he must demonstrate that he's a man and that he can perform. The wedding guests will wait outside until a bloodstained sheet has been displayed. This compulsory coupling is in fact a socially sanctioned rape as well as a blatant denial of the worth of the individual.

A marriage is never simple, but a Muslim marriage begins at the very outset with a sign of mistrust, followed by an act of force. It is in this atmosphere of mistrust and force that the next generation of children is born and brought up.

Many young Muslim women living in Western countries have devised ways to enjoy sex before marriage, while still taking into account their families' obsession with virginity. For example, they will insert foreign objects into their genitals to accomplish opportune bleeding on the night in question. They also can have their virginity "restored" if they were circumcised and had sex before marriage, a procedure that until recently was entirely reimbursed by the Dutch health insurance system. Upon a marriage proposal, a Somalian woman in Europe can have her vaginal stitches renewed by a Sudanese gynecologist in Italy; a Sudanese can go to a Somalian physician in Italy; their addresses are well known.

After marriage the mistrust of women only intensifies—now that the bride has been deflowered, her husband's fears take on even greater proportions—he has just punctured his unique means of checking whether his wife has been to bed with another man. The only way of preventing her from cheating on him is to deny her access to the outside world as much as possible. She must have his permission, or his company, for every step she takes outside the door. Supposedly, he has obtained this authority from Allah and from centuries-old traditions. The eleventh-century imam Al-Ghazzali, a scholar widely known among the orthodox, wrote: "The well brought up woman . . . doesn't leave the house, except with his definite approval, and then dressed in unattractive old clothes." And: "She always puts her husband's rights ahead of her own and that of her family. She is neat and clean and is always prepared to let him enjoy her sexually."

A good woman obeys her husband and obliges him. According to the Koran, "Men are the protectors and maintainers of women, because Allah has given the one more [strength] than the other, and because they support them from their means. Therefore, the righteous women are devoutly obedient and guard in [the husband's] absence what Allah would have them guard. As to those women on whose part ye fear disloyalty and ill-conduct, admonish them [first], [next] refuse to share their beds, [and last], chastise them [lightly] . . ." In accordance with the great and honored Caliph Umar Al-Khattab (whose status, for the Sunnis, almost equals that of the Prophet Muhammad), a woman is given three hundred lashes when four faithful Muslims testify that she has lied. Fortunately, this punishment is stretched out over three days so that the wounds are kept within bounds.

But Muslim women are only human, and from time to time they make up stories. Muslim men are not allowed to make love to a menstruating woman—the Koran says so—and this claim thereby offers excellent protection. A Muslim woman who has no desire to make love, and may become pregnant for the umpteenth time, may tell her husband that she is menstruating, a well-known excuse among Muslim women, comparable to the Western woman's "headache." Or, without her husband's knowledge, she may use contraceptives, if they are available. Some married women have abortions without telling their husbands. All this means that lies are constantly being told about the most intimate matters. It is a survival strategy, but it also becomes a way of living, and when a man discovers that his wife is lying, his suspicions that she is evil are confirmed.

Children experience their mother's lies on a daily basis. For example, if she admitted that she went out alone, her mother-in-law and her husband would be angry, so she lies. Such deceits and denials become commonplace. Admission would lead to loss of face and possibly violence. In many families, children get no allowance. A boy who steals from the household petty cash and is questioned about it does not admit the deed, for if he does he will certainly be humiliated and verbally abused. If he denies it, his honor is unblemished, and as long as he denies it, his father too can deny it to the outside world. Children learn from their mothers that it pays to lie. If they don't want to be punished they've got to come up with stories.

This "virgins' cage" has consequences for women, but also for men and children. The virgins' cage is, in fact, a double cage. Women and girls are locked up in the inner cage, but surrounding this is a larger cage in which the entire Islamic culture has been imprisoned. Caging women in order to guard their virginity leads not only to frustration and violence for the individuals directly involved, but also to socioeconomic backwardness for the entire community. These caged women actually exert a harmful influence on children, especially young boys. Since most women in the Islamic world are excluded from education, and are purposely kept ignorant, when these same women bear and raise children, they can pass on only their limited knowledge, and so perpetrate a vicious cycle of ignorance from generation to generation.

Even first-generation Muslim mothers in the West have no more than elementary education. Many are illiterate and know nothing of the society in which they have to find their way. With any luck, those who immigrated as children will become educated at a later age, but as long as the traditional sexual morality remains their parents' guiding principle for raising them, their socioeconomic progress will be difficult, if not impossible.

For many Muslims, the sexual morality of Islam has even more-far-reaching consequences. Unable to express openly the hatred they feel toward their husbands, some women direct it against their children. Of course, this does not apply to all women, for many of whom children are a consolation. But the relationship between parents and children almost never resembles what is us vidualistic society like the Netherlands.

Of course, violence against women often occurs w families, too, but Westerners emphatically repudi violence, while most Muslim families regard violence against women as something that women themselves provoke because they don't follow the rules. The family and the social environment do not disapprove of it. They reason that if your husband hits you, it must be because you had it coming to you. Western neighbors, family members, and friends don't believe that the mistreatment of women is an acceptable educational device.

The Koran assigns great importance to values such as trust, truthfulness, and learning. Yet in just the few examples I have recounted above we can see how things actually stand in daily Islamic life—it is a dismal state of affairs. Mistrust is everywhere, and lies rule.

In order to put Islam's strict sexual morality into perspective, we need to examine and analyze its practical consequences. Relations between the sexes have to be described objectively and critically. Then, on the basis of the resulting data, proposals must be made for changing the way in which men and women relate to each other.

The United Nations reports suggest that the systematic gathering of knowledge is not valued in the Arabic-Islamic countries. According to the Koran, the faithful must ceaselessly strive after knowledge, but the Koran also states that Allah is all-knowing and that the Koran is the source of all knowledge. It is impossible to reconcile these two positions. For Muslim children the study of biology and history can be very confusing. After all, history begins in a time before the Koran begins, and the theory of evolution contradicts the creation story in the Koran. Most mullahs advise Muslims who are confounded by this contradictory state of affairs that, when the Koran speaks of the "search for knowledge," it means that a Muslim must keep on reading the Koran until, as a result of this dedicated reading, gateways to knowledge open by themselves.

The values of the Koran are essentially unattainable for any human being. A great tension exists between the inhumanly strict demands that Islam makes on the faithful and what they are able to live up to. Young men or women may want to meet the demand to remain virgins until marriage, but their hormones give them inclinations and thoughts that conflict with that demand and are therefore considered sinful. Along with the realization that the strict prescriptions of the Koran cannot be put into practice come doubts. Yet one is not allowed to doubt either the Koran or the Sunna (a collection of traditions about the life of Muhammad). After all, Muhammad's life was exemplary. Doubt is immediately punishable, if not by the social environment, then by Allah. But without doubts, without a standpoint reached through questioning, human beings can't acquire knowledge. Consequently, even ardent followers of Islam find themselves in a precarious dilemma.

Because of this inner impasse, Muslim women and men often become confused; a community that lives according to the prescriptions of Muhammad and the Koran inevitably becomes pathological in its fears of contradictions, in its anger at inner and outside questioning, and in its frustrations at never being able to fulfill the ideals that they are taught to live up to. But many Muslims refuse to attribute responsibility for their misery to their own community or to the sexual morality imposed by their religion. Instead, they blame Allah, the Devil, or other external sources such as the Jews, Americans, or colonialism. Muslims don't recognize that, in fact, the pursuit of a life based on their own Holy Book is the most significant source of their unhappiness.

A large number of Muslims, however, do manage to cope through denial. They say, *I'm absolutely not going to ask my wife whether she is a virgin. I don't care. I'll leave that to Allah.* And that way they survive.

TO BREAK OUT of the cage in which Muslims are imprisoned and in which they've imprisoned their women, they must start to practice self-criticism and test the moral values they derive from the Koran. The 15 million Muslims who live in the West are in the best position to do this because of civil rights and liberties, with freedom of expression not the least among them. A Muslim in Europe who closely examines the foundations of his faith does not have to fear a prison sentence or, as in the Arabic-Islamic countries, the death penalty. Ni Putes Ni Soumises ("Neither whores nor submissives"), the group of Muslim women in France that is protesting against gang rapes committed by fellow Muslims, is an example of a group making use of their freedom of expression. The leader of this group, Samira Bellil, was herself a victim of gang rape. A comparable protest is virtually impossible in any Islamic country. Another example is the pamphlet "Off with the Veil!" by the Iranian Chahdortt Djavann. In Iran, where wearing the veil is obligatory, this pamphlet would never even have been published. Several other writers and thinkers with Islamic backgrounds are also taking advantage of Western liberties, for example, the novelist Hafid Bouazza and the philosopher Afshin Ellian, who both work in the Netherlands. Maybe one day their work will be translated into Arabic and Persian, but for now it is banned in most Islamic countries. Perhaps the writer who has best identified the problems within the Muslim world is the philosopher Ibn Warraq, of Pakistani origin, author of *Why I Am Not a Muslim*. That this courageous man writes under a pseudonym shows that even in the West he does not feel safe.

Muslims who live in the West have easier access to information, and particularly the long tradition of religious criticism in the West. They can gather knowledge from not only libraries and in universities, but also from other people, and they can start to take a critical look at their own faith.

Self-criticism for Muslims is possible in the West, because the West, primarily the United States, is waging war on Islamic terrorism. Paradoxically, the attacks of September 11 have led to an enormous fascination with Islam. This fascination—which admittedly stems in part from an instinct for self-preservation—gives Muslims in the West an unusual opportunity to escape from their psychological cage.

In spite of these favorable circumstances, however, many Western Muslims are still more strongly influenced by conservative Islamic thought than by the ideas of sociologist Fatima Mernissi, for instance, the author of *Beyond the Veil: Male-Female Dynamics in Modern Muslim Society,* and a scientist who has been influenced by Western thought. Of course, I recognize that not all 15 million Muslims are ready to adopt a critical standpoint with respect to the Prophet, and that some of them will resort to threats and intimidation, perhaps even taking the law into their own hands and committing murder. But I do find it startling that many women still strongly resist change, for example, by demonstratively wearing the *hijab.* Many women say that they didn't wear a *hijab* in Turkey but started doing so after their arrival in the Netherlands. This reactionary attitude has a disheartening effect on progressive European Muslims.

THERE ARE THREE kinds of Muslims in the West. The first is a silent minority that doesn't live according to the prescriptions of Islam and clearly understands that the future rests with individualism. These people silently take leave of Islam. They work hard and, when they can afford it, they move to better neighborhoods; they send their children to university and don't get mixed up in the current heated discussion in the West about Islam.

A second group feels greatly hurt by external criticism of their faith and takes it personally. For generations these Muslims have accepted that the blame for their distress lies outside themselves and outside the Koran and the Prophet Muhammad.

Finally there are the progressive Muslims. This group consists of individuals who say, "Let's examine ourselves and try to figure out what's wrong." They want to take the cage apart piece by piece and enable more people to escape it. But these attempts to liberate Muslims in the West are being frustrated by vehemently negative reactions from, of all people, secular Westerners. The few enlightened Muslims run into direct opposition from Western cultural relativists who say, "It's part of the culture; you shouldn't detract from that." Or "If you criticize Islam, you hurt your people, and that makes you a racist or Islamophobe." I have even been called an enlightenment fundamentalist, which I took to mean that I am just as radical in my commitment to individual rights—as if that were negative—as the Islamic fundamentalists are committed to religious doctrine. Because of this, the cage persists. A type of satanic pact has been forged between Westerners who make their living by representing Muslim interests, extending aid to them, and cooperating with them in their development, and Muslims who have a vested interest in the cage—a myopic, selfish, short-term interest.

Five years ago I was still one of the silent minority; I believed that I was living in a free country. I thought that if a woman is beaten and tolerates that, she is responsible for her own misfortune. I thought if I were her, I'd run away. I would not have my hymen restored. I would start my own life over, in the here and now. But today, I think differently. I now see how important upbringing is, not only because that is how one's life starts but also because in Islamic culture that is how the cage is built. Psychological conditioning is very powerful, and it takes great energy and force of mind and will to break out of it. Many Muslim girls are brought up according to the Koran and the example of the Prophet Muhammad, to live subserviently and submissively. It is very difficult for them to liberate themselves from this cage when they are older. Every Muslim is expected to submit to the will of Allah, but the girls and women have to submit most of all. This upbringing can have so great an influence that women never succeed in escaping from the cage. Because they have internalized their subordination, they no longer experience it as an oppression by an external force but as a strong internal shield. Women who have mastered the survival strategies derive a certain pride from living this way. They are like prisoners suffering from Stockholm syndrome, in which hostages fall in love with the hostage takers and establish a deep, intimate contact with them. But it is an unhealthy intimacy, comparable to slaves who are subordinate not only in body, but also psychologically, and who preferred the certainty of their existence in slavery to a freedom that they perceive as treacherous.

When I visited with the women of the Turkish movement Milli Görüs, I found them assertive and clamorous, almost to the point of being aggressive. They angrily defended their own oppression: "I *want* to wear a *hijab*, I *want* to obey my husband." I have also met Moroccan women who said: "I want to wear the *hijab*, because Allah the Exalted has commanded it." "Well," I respond, "if you want to do everything that Allah the Exalted has said, then you'll stay in your cage."

Meanwhile, many are waiting for an enlightenment to take place in Islam. But that enlightenment won't come by itself. That is why the way in which Muslims think about Islam has to change. Muslims need to think differently about how they deal with their faith, about life, about giving meaning to life, and about their own sexual morality. The few Muslims who have gained their individuality can hold up a mirror to the community from which they have emerged to make them face their still-undeveloped individuality, to make them see the "I" that is constantly being oppressed and curbed by dogma, prescriptions, and the stifling culture of gossip that rules in most Islamic communities. Emancipation doesn't mean the liberation of the community of the faithful or its safeguarding from the power of evil outside forces, such as colonialism, capitalism, the Jews, and the Americans. It means the liberation of the individual from that same community of the faithful. And to liberate him- or herself as an individual, he or she must first come to think differently about sexuality.

The best way for Islamic culture to liberate itself from its backwardness is by ceasing to blame others for that backwardness. Muslim men and women must carefully, thoughtfully reevaluate their current sexual morality and their adherence to Islamic moral guidance. They must also determine how the prescribed morality is actually practiced; what are its real-life consequences and results. For instance, how many people succeed in living up to the standard that everyone must enter into marriage virginal and pure, the way Allah wants it, according to the Koran? How do men and women actually relate to one another in the real world, in day-to-day life? To what extent are family violence and violence against women unintended consequences of the striving after an unattainable ideal that is meant to secure an agreeable place in the afterlife? Is overpopulation and the rise of sexually transmitted diseases, especially AIDS, in Islamic countries a direct consequence of the existing sexual morality? What about the rise in the number of abortions among Muslims in the West?

Instead of devoting their energy and money to the development of an even larger atomic bomb—as Pakistan and Iran are doing—the Islamic world would be better employed in critically examining its own sexual morality and the suffocating effects of its own cultures and societies, and devising proposals for change.

Scientific and scholarly research are necessary but not sufficient to overcome the cultural challenges in making large groups of people change their position. Almost all books about Islam written by Muslims are educational texts and guides instructing Muslims on how to behave in accordance with the precepts in the Koran and the Hadith, theological studies with little that is creative or new. Alongside these there are novels by Muslims about love, politics, and crime, in which the role of Islam and the Prophet Muhammad are studiously avoided, although the moral undercurrent is that one should observe religious precepts, otherwise things end very badly. Most Islamic soaps, broadcast around the world via satellite, share not only their bad acting but also an adherence to Islamic sexual morality in relationships between the main characters. The message is that if a young man and young woman choose each other out of love they will come to a bad end; if they come together because their families have arranged it, then everything will end well, with a splendid wedding, mounds of gold, and tears of joy.

What Muslim culture needs instead of this pablum, however, are books, soap operas, poetry, and songs that depict what is really happening and that satirize religious precepts, such as those presented in *Customs and Morals in Islam* and *Guide to Islamic Upbringing,* books that have been translated from Arabic into Dutch and distributed in Holland. Satire is a bitter necessity; it has to happen. The book *A Glimpse of Hell,* which tells us what awaits us in the hereafter, could be beautifully parodied in a film. As soon as something like Monty Python's *The Life of Brian* appears with a Muhammad figure as the main lead, directed by an Arabic Theo van Gogh, the controversial late Dutch filmmaker, we will have taken an enormous step forward. I want to see Muhammad, *with* his nine wives, appear in a film like *Ben-Hur.* Arabic poets often think that they can write much better than Shakespeare. But if this is the case, where is the Islamic *Romeo and Juliet*? And where is the Moroccan Madonna who will sing *Like a Prayer*? Is a director like David Potter, who makes a film in which an Arabic woman's lipstick ends up on the collar of an Iranian general, even imaginable in the Islamic world?

Steps toward modernization are being taken in Turkey, Morocco, Indonesia, and other countries, but champions of modernization will meet a lot of resistance from those Muslim brothers and sisters who would prefer to spend a few more centuries in the virgins' cage. Native Westerners themselves have an important task: they must not allow themselves to be tempted to protect the "injured" Muslims. It is in the interest of the Islamic world *and* of the Western world to promote a flourishing culture of self-criticism among Muslims and to support it wherever possible. The Islamic world is in a great crisis that also constitutes a threat to the West, a threat that consists not only of terrorism but also of streams of migration and of the risk that civil wars will break out in the Middle East—the greatest source of oil for the West. Such a threat can only be lessened when the Muslim world reforms itself from the inside, with assistance from the West. A reform of the Islamic world is in the interests of both.

FOUR

Let Us Have a Voltaire

Nobody who has been following the debates since September 11—in the newspapers, on television, and in political arena—can have failed to notice the sharp rise in criticism of Islam throughout the West. The main question people ask is whether Islam in its present form is compatible with the system of constitutional democracy. Should Islam embark on a period of enlightenment and modernization? Does Islam need a Voltaire to call Muslims to break free of superstition, to use their minds and not their emotions, to take note, as he did in the 1800s, that "Nothing can be more contrary to religion and the clergy than reason and common sense." And, "The truths of religion are never so well understood as by those who have lost their power of reasoning." Is there an enlightened Muslim man or woman who can stand with Voltaire and say, "To think of virginity as a virtue—and not a barrier that separates ignorance from knowledge—is an infantile superstition"? Where is the biting criticism of Islam from within? Or is it the West that should be listening to the critical voice of Voltaire and examining itself and its commitment to its moral principles? As Thomas L. Friedman has written, Westerners should hold Arabs and Muslims to the same high moral standards as Westerners hold for themselves.

In order to answer the question of compatibility between present-day Islam and Western culture, it makes sense to compare the two worlds.

Islamic fundamentalism and political Islam have not suddenly appeared out of nowhere. They needed a breeding ground, where they could take root and grow, before they were transformed into the very dangerous forms that have confronted us since September 11. This breeding ground is created by the way Islam is taught, day in day out, to Muslims in the Islamic world. No matter how great the diversity within the Muslim community, it is the teaching of Islam, and the way people apply its doctrines to real life, that prepares the ground for the growth of fundamentalism and, ultimately, terrorism.

The writer Leon de Winter, best known for his argument that a third World War is going on between the West and terrorists, points to a number of bad practices that take place in some Islamic countries. Although I do not share his opinion of a third World War, his description of the Islamic world is surprisingly accurate. For a start, de Winter gives an excellent description of the ideology that fueled the terrorists of September 11 and their followers. Their religious ideological framework consists of "strength and weakness, dominance and humiliation, eternity and transience, clarity and obscurity," and they justify their actions and attribute them to divine justice.

From my own experience, I can confirm that the Islamic world is divided according to a strict hierarchy. Allah is almighty, and man is His slave and must obey His laws. Those who believe what is written in the Koran, who believe in Allah and accept Muhammad as His prophet, are superior to other religious peoples. Practicing Muslims are "tribes of the Scriptures" and are also superior to those whose beliefs have lapsed and to nonbelievers. Men come before women, and children must obey their parents. People who break these rules must be humiliated or murdered in the name of God.

Life on earth is temporary. It offers believers a chance to prove their fear of God through the strict observation of their duties to Him, which will earn them a place in heaven. Nonbelievers merely serve as examples of how not to lead your life. *Halal* (that which is permitted) and *haram* (that which is forbidden) are the two central concepts underlying everyday life. They apply to all Muslims, any-where in the world, and affect all areas of life. Fixed rules describe exactly how to think, feel, and act, and what to avoid and apply equally to the private and public domains of Muslim life. The *Shari'a,* or Islamic law, comes before any law or rule instituted by people. And it is every Muslim's duty to follow the *Shari'a* as strictly as possible. Fundamentalists take advantage of this expectation by pointing out, again and again, that moderate Muslims do not live their lives according to Islamic doctrine.

From our early years, we Muslims learn all this from our parents, in the mosques and the madrassas (schools for the study of Koran, which have become in many countries schools for fundamentalist Islamists). In addition, Muslims in Europe and the United States receive special tuition through the writings of people like Yusuf al-Qaradawi, whom some regard as a moderate Muslim theologian and a suitable discussion partner for the West. Actually, al-Qaradawi's views are far from moderate. In his book *The Lawful and the Prohibited in Islam*—aimed exclusively at Western Muslims—he writes that the Islamic community has a duty to acquire military skills so that it will be ready to defend itself against the enemies of God and safeguard the honor of Islam. According to al-Qaradawi, Muslims who fail to do this are committing a severe sin. A little further on in the book he mentions that all laws drawn up by people are inadequate and incomplete, since the legislators have restricted themselves to material matters only, neglecting the demands of religion and morality. It is difficult for a non-Muslim to grasp how severely this statement undermines the democratic process of legislation in the eyes of "Westernized" Muslim readers.

De Winter aptly describes the practical experience of Islam as a daily drama in which "rows of saints, ghosts, angels, and little demons play significant supporting parts. The conservative Muslim thus accepts that his enemies may have supernatural powers with which to hatch plots, and, of course, the average Muslim does not know how to deal with such powers." In this context de Winter quotes the Israeli professor Emmanuel Sivan, who conducted a study of fundamentalism: "A world inhabited by ghosts, the spirits of the dead, and *jinn* (invisible creatures), some evil and some good; a world besieged by the magic of a seducing Satan and his demons, where holy men and angels, and if necessary miracles, free the believer; a world in which communication with the dead (in particular of one's own family) is an everyday occurrence, and where the presence of the supernatural is regarded as an almost tangible reality."

As a Muslim I recognize these descriptions. All over the world Muslims are brought up with similar beliefs in the supernatural. Everything in day-to-day life is geared toward the existence of a hereafter. It's a short step from these beliefs to the belief that we earn a place in paradise through martyrdom, a mind-set far removed from reason. It would be very interesting to examine to what extent superstition and the lack of common sense in the practice of Islam is linked to the wide appeal of Bin Laden's ideology among Muslims. He appeals to the colorful fantasies and dreams of Muslims who do not want to take responsibility for their own state and for their own deeds, those who shift blame for their country's and their own problems onto outside "authorities"—onto the West, onto the United States.

Many madrassas imbue their pupils with an irrational hatred of Jews and an aversion to nonbelievers, a message that is also frequently repeated in the mosques. Jews are consistently portrayed as the instigators of evil in books, on cassette tapes, and by the media. I myself experienced how insidious the effects of years of this indoctrination can be: the first time I saw a Jew with my own eyes, I was surprised to find a human being of flesh and blood.

De Winter writes that the current anger felt by many Muslims—which has given rise to strong anti-American sentiments and speculations about plots—does not merely have its roots in the socioeconomic poverty of Muslims relative to Christians and Jews. "The anger also comes from an irrational and conservative religious experience, in which Satan is alive." I would like to take de

Winter's argument further and emphasize that this kind of religious experience is common not only among radical Muslims and fundamentalists, but also among ordinary Muslims. The difference is that the fanatics do not stop at hatred and are prepared to commit acts of terror.

All Muslims learn to regard our life on earth as an investment in the hereafter by obeying God's will and His laws. The values of the community—honor and submission—are of much greater importance than the individual's autonomy. Religion is not considered a tool with which the individual can add meaning to his life or not use at all. It is an absolute. The individual is expected to accept his religion and to devote himself to God in accordance with the literal meaning of the word *Islam:* submission to God's will.

Many who grow up and live with Islamic traditions, and who are susceptible to fundamentalism and radicalism, tend to be passive in life and to be guided by a sense of fatalism. A practicing Muslim who tries to become an integrated member of Western society is in a difficult position. A Muslim immigrant in the West is confronted with a world turned upside down.

Unlike Islamic society, the West places much emphasis on the individual's independence and personal responsibility, and on the necessity of investing in this life. Education and employment, rather than piety, are a measure of success. Western societies are not dominated by one single ideology, but have several ideologies that exist alongside one another. In a well-functioning democracy, the state constitution is considered more important than God's holy book, whichever holy book that may be, and God matters only in your private life. Relationships between people and their interactions are governed by laws and rules, which were drawn up by people, not divine forces, and can be changed, adapted, or replaced by new ones. All people are the same in the face of the law, even those whose lifestyles differ from that of the majority. Women have equal opportunities under the law (although in reality this is not always so). Homosexuality is not a sin to be punished with death, nor is it considered a threat to the survival of mankind, but seen as a form of love, normal like that between heterosexuals. Moreover, love and sex are not restricted to marriage, but can be enjoyed between two people by mutual consent. Democracy provides the freedom to avoid or plan a pregnancy and ways to protect against sexually transmitted diseases.

In the West, Muslims can see that Jews are not monsters who are hostile to Islam, who want to be at war with them, destroy their hope, and spread fear, but ordinary people with a shocking history of their own in Europe—the Holocaust. In the West, prosperity and misfortune are not the products of God's will, but of human action. Society can be shaped; you can influence your surroundings. And the hereafter is of little consequence. Anyone who wishes to believe in it should decide so for himself, but no official or state involvement is necessary or required. Many things that are forbidden in Islam are appreciated in Western societies, while in the West many Muslim duties are dismissed and thought to be backward.

Very few Muslims are actually capable of looking at their faith critically. Critical minds like those of Afshin Ellian in the Netherlands and Salman Rushdie in England are exceptions. Instead of self-criticism, we are offered a series of denials, or a list of external factors, and plots, that are the "true causes" of everything that has gone wrong in the Muslim world. Muslims are defensive, even to criticism of Islamists responsible for 9/11. And many Western thinkers and politicians exacerbate this Muslim tendency to avoid internal reflection by themselves avoiding looking at Islam. They lean back complacently and opine: "Oh, well, it was like that with us once. The Church governed the West in the Dark Ages. Don't worry, all will be fine with Islam in the end." They do not know what they're talking about.

Present-day Islam is not compatible with the expectations of Western states. Islam is in need of enlightenment. Islamic societies still wrestle with the problems of the Dark Ages (prejudice, restricted thought, superstition) that strapped Christian societies before the Reformation and the Age of Reason questioned central tenets. But it is unlikely that this movement will rise up from within the Islamic world. Writers, academics, and journalists who voice their criticism are forced to take refuge in the West. Their works are banned in their own country.

What, then, can Westerners do? At an international level, leaders such as Blair and Bush must stop saying that Islam is being held hostage by a terrorist minority. They are wrong. Islam is being held hostage by itself. It would be more useful if they confronted Saudi Arabia with the fact that its repressive regime, its demographic pressure, and its biased religious education system have created a breeding ground for extremists. Almost five years after 9/11, they have been addressed to only a small extent.

In the Netherlands and elsewhere in Europe, the native white majority can help the Islamic minority by not trivializing the seriousness of the present crisis in Islam. By addressing absolutist attitudes toward the Koran and the infallibility of the Prophet Muhammad, Muslims in the West can learn from the questions and criticisms that have been put to Islam since September 11. More pressure should be put on minorities to become fully integrated into local and state cultures. Democracies should foster the voices of dissent and sponsor Muslim dissidents in the West, so that the one-sided, stultifying religious rhetoric to which millions of Muslims are subjected every day has a counterpoint.

Let the Muslim Voltaires of today work in a safe environment on the enlightenment of Islam, which will lead to an international enlightenment, as the power of reason and individual responsibility frees the minds of individual Muslims of the burden of the hereafter, the constant feelings of guilt, and the temptation of fundamentalism. We would learn to feel responsible for our problems and the areas in which we lag behind. Let us have a Voltaire.

FIVE

What Went Wrong?

A Modern Clash of Cultures

Immigrants are expected to adopt certain standards and values that are part and parcel of Western society and to behave accordingly. The debate around integration denounces the behavior of Muslims who do not meet these standards but often fails to tackle the underlying causes. Westerners condemn polygamy, vendetta, and abuse of women; we want to improve education and increase employment; we see the causal link between unfinished school careers and criminality. And yet we prefer not to discuss the cultural and religious backgrounds of these wrongs and problems. We readily pass over the fact that traditional customs and orthodox religious opinions stand in the way of integration.

It is clear that "old forms and thoughts" will continue to influence Muslims for a long time to come. Archconservative imams, marriage to imported partners, the increased interest in Islamic teachings, and watching TV stations with fundamentalist leanings all contribute to this. Western integration policy should therefore address the regrettable correlation between the limited cultural development of large sections of the Muslim population and their social disadvantages.

The basic principles of traditional Islam, combined with the old customs of the ethnic groups, clash with the elementary values and standards of Western society. Failing to adopt the values of the host society or adhering to the standards of the country of origin explains

to a large extent why many Muslims in the Netherlands are falling behind socially and economically. With the help of the work of three
writers—Karen Armstrong, Bernard Lewis, and David Pryce-Jones—
I argue that the Islamic faith lends itself more than any other to the
preservation of premodern customs and traditions. For in Islam, culture and religion are very closely connected, and verses from the
Koran legitimize many practices that—in the eyes of Westerners—
are unacceptable. The mental world of Islam is a reflection of the
stagnation that entrapped this religion a few centuries after its birth.

This premodern mentality will continue to work against Muslim
integration in the West. But there are four different models to solve
the problems of integration: the political-legal model, the (purely)
socioeconomic model, the multicultural model, and the sociocultural model. To a greater or lesser extent, each takes into account
the cultural-religious background of Muslim immigrants.

SOCIAL RELEVANCE

Of course, immigrants from Surinam, the Antilles, (Christian)
Ghana, and China (to name but a few groups) also have problems,
but Muslims have very specific difficulties that stem from religion
and culture when it comes to adjusting to a modern, Western society. This is "religion as a culture-forming factor, with a system of
values and morals derived from ideas about Divine Truth, and on
the basis of this, a community, which is a natural translation of a
higher moral order." The drop in the number of young Muslims
who attend the mosque by no means implies that these young people do not regard themselves as Muslims. For many nonpracticing
Muslims, the essence of their identity and the system of values and
morals by which they live remain Islamic.

Muslims in the Netherlands and other Western European countries are immigrants from Turkey and Morocco who have come to
find work and have had children there. In the year 2000 these Dutch
communities counted 309,000 and 262,000 registered people, re-

spectively. In addition, the past decade has seen a considerable influx of asylum seekers, from Iraq (38,000), Somalia (30,000), Afghanistan (26,000), and Iran (24,000). In 2000 a total of approximately 35,000 people had arrived in the Netherlands from Pakistan, Tunisia, and Algeria. As a consequence of family reunion and childbirth, these communities are expected to increase dramatically over the next few decades. A few facts:

- Muslims now form the biggest ideological category within the immigrant community. In absolute figures this means 736,000 Muslims. Most Muslims remain strongly focused on their own communities and have a very high proportion of marriages to foreign Islamic partners (almost three-quarters of Turkish and Moroccan marriages) as opposed to the low proportion of marriages to native Dutch partners (probably under 5 percent). "The vast majority, especially those who come from Islamic countries, do not converge. . . . Their demographic profile is traditional, and what is particularly striking is that the first and second generations seem no different in this respect." The preservation of old customs (such as marrying and having children early) in a modern society becomes a substantial obstacle to social mobility and integration. And the children from these families with parents who have had little or no education will follow in their parents' footsteps. "And of course your social mobility depends very much on having been in education for a certain period of time, which is in conflict with marrying young and having children early."

- Muslims in the Netherlands reside predominantly in the deprived areas of the big and middle-sized cities. They are generally poorly educated. The majority of Turks and Moroccans come from the lowest socioeconomic strata in their native countries. A good proportion of asylum seekers has scarcely any education. The dropout rate from schools among Muslim children is relatively high. Even girls who go on to higher education are forced into marriage by their families and will often break off their education. Unemployment among Muslims is still two to three times higher than among the native population. Those who do have jobs often work in areas sensitive to economic fluctuations such as retail and catering. Their dependence on social welfare is relatively high. Crime rates are disproportionately high. Frank Bovenkerk and Yucel Yesilgöz even call these figures alarming.

- Since the attacks of 9/11 and the results of the May 15, 2002 election (the national parliamentary elections in the Netherlands)—the main issue of which was the integration of minorities and the integration of Muslims into Dutch society—the question of Muslim integration has become more urgent. The tone of the discussions is turning grimmer, and in the media much attention is given to the radical political dimension of Islam, to which Muslims in the Netherlands, as elsewhere in the West, seem susceptible.

THE WORLD OF ISLAM

In their effort to understand Islam, researchers often separate the religion from its social origins. They describe the theological diversity within Islam, recount its philosophical history, or portray Islam as a spiritual inner journey. Hardly anyone has analyzed the origins of this world religion from a sociological point of view.

This is not surprising, given the fact that Islam had no real presence in Western Europe until recently and was a subject for research only among an exclusive, small circle of classical orientalists whose methods and personal interests colored their findings. There is also very little sociological research into Islam by established Muslim academics.

Lewis and Pryce-Jones discuss three closely linked characteristics of the mental world of traditional Islam. According to them, the religious-cultural identity of Muslims is characterized by:

- A hierarchical-authoritarian mentality: "The boss is almighty; others can only obey."

- Group identity: "The group always comes before the individual"; if you do not belong to the clan/tribe you will be treated with suspicion or, at best, not be taken seriously.

- A patriarchal mentality and culture of shame: The woman has a reproductive function and must obey the male members of her family; failure to do so brings shame on the family.

The Islamic identity (view of mankind and the world) is based on groups, and its central concepts are honor and disgrace, or shame. "Honor" is closely linked to the group. The relevant groups, in order of size, are the family, the clan, the tribe, and, ultimately, the community of the faithful *(ummah)*.

Within the community of the faithful, the fact that someone claims to be a Muslim is enough for other Muslims to regard that person as closer to them than any non-Muslim. Muslims feel an emotional bond with their oppressed brothers and sisters elsewhere in the world. When a group of Muslims—no matter where—is suffering or being oppressed (Kashmir, Palestine), the community of the faithful is commonly depicted as a bleeding body in pain.

Within the tribe or race, a person from the same region or country is closer to you than anyone from a faraway country. This does not necessarily imply sharing the same nationality (a modern concept). A Turkish Kurd feels kindred to a Kurd from Iran or Iraq, and—because of an extended history of war and hostilities—*not* to his Turkish neighbors.

Within the family and the (sub)clan circles, it is a source of honor to have as many sons as possible. This is why men often marry young and will have more than one wife. The subordinate position of women is a consequence of the cultural desire to have many sons. There are two reasons. First, children always adopt their father's name and never their mother's (i.e., *her* father's name).

When the woman marries someone outside the subclan and has children, she serves the interests of the rival subclan. Because of the distrust of rival (sub)clans (you never know, they might grow stronger and more aggressive and attack you), it is customary to encourage marriage among cousins. The wish to have so many sons can lead to an uncontrollable surge in the population. And marrying family members comes with considerable health risks for the offspring.

Second, a woman can tarnish her father's honor, and consequently that of his clan, often incurring dreadful repercussions. She may do this by wearing the wrong kind of clothing outside the home or by going out with a boyfriend before marriage. Punishments include verbal warnings, physical abuse, expulsion, and even murder. The outcome is almost invariably that no man will subsequently want to marry her. Not only does the family lose status, but the woman remains a financial burden. Her presence in the parental home is a permanent reminder of the shame she has brought upon her family and the clan. In other words, the individual is completely subordinate to the collective. Every child has to learn its social skills in a culture of shame, which centers on the concepts of honor and disgrace. There is no room whatsoever for the values of freedom and individual responsibility in this way of thinking. The first rule a child is taught is to obey the adults in his or her family. Boys, moreover, learn from a very early age to give as good as they get. Aggressive behavior is functional in this culture and serves the purpose of avoiding public humiliation by others.

This premodern culture closely resembles a concept called the General Human Pattern (GHP), a pattern that was found in all societies at one time, except today's. In this model developed by Dutch philosopher Jan Romein, man feels that he is part of nature; he wants to use it without feeling an obsessive need to scrutinize all its secrets. The GHP mind thinks in a particular way: concrete rather than abstract; it resorts to images rather than concepts. Conscious organization and planning play a much less important role for him than in modern societies. In the GHP mind, power and authority are absolute and unassailable. Anyone who opposes the authorities is punished. Finally, work as a necessary function in society in this mind-set is not regarded as a blessing, but as a curse and a burden. Doing nothing is a luxury desired by all but granted to only a few.

ISLAM AND THE TRIBAL MENTALITY

Islam began in a tribal society. The monotheism of Islam marked a sharp break with the polytheism that had prevailed on the Arabian Peninsula until then. The new faith inspired Muhammad's tribe in its constant battle to fend off neighboring tribes. Muhammad preached charity: once conquered, tribes were not enslaved if they converted to Islam and joined in the battle against nonbelieving tribes. This gave the Muslim religion a strongly expansionist character: much importance is attributed to the conquest and conversion of those who do not believe in Allah. Islam adopted some pre-Islamic spiritual traditions, such as praying, fasting, and giving alms. The relationship between Muhammad and his god is vertical: God is almighty, He is one, and Muhammad obeys His commands. The relationship between Muhammad and his followers is simple and the same: Muhammad's will is the law.

The Koran prescribes the ideal ordering of society with rules primarily designed to bring under control the tribal anarchy of the time, with its extremely violent fights against and among clans and tribes. In *The Closed Circle,* David Pryce-Jones describes how this tribal system functioned. In a vicious cycle of violence, one tribe tried to dominate another, which meant that there was a permanent struggle for power within the tribe, the clan, and the family. At the top of every family, clan, or tribe stood one man. Often this captain had acquired his position through cunning and violence. For instance, Muhammad had managed to get a number of tribes to accept important political and social (and eventually also economic) regulations that supported values central to the tribal way of life, such as maintaining the tribe's honor and the redistribution of property. These laws brought a lasting solution to the problems between rival tribes and forced them to become allies. The fighting continued, but only against tribes outside the Islamic circle.

Not surprisingly, many of the laws laid down by the Koran put the social peace of the group first, within which there is a high degree of social control. Many of these laws are related to the honor of a man, his family, or his clan. The opposite of honor is disgrace, so a man is as passionate about guarding his honor as he is about avoiding shame and disgrace. Lies and evasion play an important part in this culture of honor and shame; ignoring or simply denying what has really happened is normal. The tribal culture has a strongly developed sense of mistrust, not only of outsiders, but also of the members of one's own family or clan.

RISE AND FALL OF ISLAM

Islam united ignorant Arabic tribes that had been deeply immersed in anarchy into a world civilization. In the seventh century, Muslims conquered Syria, Palestine, Egypt, and the rest of North Africa and began to move into the Iberian Peninsula. Nothing seemed to stop the new faith from spreading. During the rise of Islam, the only other civilization of a comparable standard and size was China. But Bernard Lewis distinguishes the Chinese civilization from Islam because it was restricted to a single region and one racial group. The Muslims created a multiethnic, multiracial, and universal world civilization. Yet today, compared with the Christian West, the Muslim world has become poor, weak, fractious, and ignorant.

According to Lewis, the question "What went wrong?" is commonly tackled from either a secular or sociopsychological point of view. Secularists put the role of religion in Islamic society at the center of the discussion and argue that the West's economic and cultural primacy is the result of the separation of church and state and of the institution of a civil society that follows secular legislation. The others, especially feminists, focus on sexism and the inferior position of women in Islamic society. Not only do these problems deprive the Islamic world of half their population's talents and energy, they disadvantage their own children by leaving them in the care of illiterate, downtrodden mothers.

"The products of such an education . . . are likely to grow up arrogant or submissive, and unfit for a free, open society," says Lewis. Indeed a growing number of Muslims claim the answer to "What went wrong?" is that they have been struck by evil because of their neglect of the divine inheritance of Islam. This all too simple response is fatal to further economic development because it means a return to a largely imaginary past as occurred in the Iranian Revolution and in other fundamentalist movements and regimes in Muslim countries. In comparison, the secular system of democracy offers more opportunities. Some historical thinkers, Lewis among them, are optimistic about Kemal Atatürk's Turkish Republic. Others, including Pryce-Jones, are less optimistic about the extent to which secularism and other Western developments are (or can be) truly understood by people who are used to living in a tribal society.

Lewis's position is unambiguous. The subtitle of his book, *The Clash Between Islam and Modernity in the Middle East,* is revealing. The people who abandoned Islamic civilization have not fully experienced the intrusive, painful but ultimately liberating process of modernization as their neighbors and rivals in the Christian West have. Lewis warns that a downward spiral of hatred and resentment, anger and self-pity, poverty and oppression can result from rejecting modernity, but he hopes that Muslims will use their talents and energy to achieve a common goal, so that one day Islamic nations may become an important civilization again.

In this respect Lewis is more optimistic than Pryce-Jones. Lewis demands that Muslims relinquish their most substantial values, the things they pass on to their children including the patriarchal family structure and the mind-set that is obsessed with honor and group self-image. But, as Pryce-Jones says, these are the very characteristics that define the tribe, precisely the attributes that make it such a tightly closed community. These tribal values, and the sense of identity that accompanies them, are so deeply ingrained that the people have become blind to their disastrous long-term effects. The total acceptance of these values is perpetuated by the endlessly repeated processes, that legitimized premodern concepts with texts from the Koran. The ideas and traditions of Muhammad's tribal society are adopted straight into the industrial and urban society of today, without any consideration for their historical context.

The historian Karen Armstrong believes that in the past Muslims have successfully demonstrated they can separate reason from religion. After all, Muslims once had great philosophers and created a world civilization. She feels that the problem is not so much rooted in Muslims themselves, and their religion, as in the West's attitude toward Muslim countries. Imperialism and the supremacy of the United States as a trading power have deprived Muslims of the opportunity to come to grips with their own problems.

Lewis is more skeptical. He agrees that from the nineteenth century onward the British and French came to dominate the Islamic people both politically and economically. This brought about some fundamental cultural changes, such as the migration to cities in the twentieth century. Neither does he dispute that this development transformed the lives of Muslims, in both a positive and a negative sense. He acknowledges that the Americans have strategic interests to protect in the region (securing the stability of their oil supply). Yet, according to Lewis, none of this is the real cause of the lack of progress in Islamic countries. Rather, these are the consequences, just as the Mongolian invasion during the thirteenth century was possible only because the Islamic empire was suffering from internal weakness at the time.

Both Lewis and Pryce-Jones believe that the main reason for the decline lies in the inability of Muslims to set up democratic institutions that safeguard the right to individual freedom, put the relative values of scientific knowledge and religious wisdom into perspective (scientific research is often brought to a halt when it is perceived as a threat to religious dogmas), and undo the social and psychological consequences of the subjugation of women. They do not say in so many words that Islam as a religion is at the root of the tragic situation in large parts of the Islamic world, but their analysis does point to the fact that the dominance of religious practice in the Muslim world (among orthodox followers and fundamentalists) forms a serious obstacle to social progress and emancipation for all Muslims.

In July 2002 the United Nations Development Program published the *Arab Human Development Report,* an analytical survey of the average life expectancy, the level of education, and the standard of life of the inhabitants of twenty-two Islamic countries. The report confirms the theory put forward by Pryce-Jones and Lewis: deep-rooted institutional shortcomings stand in the way of human development. According to the report, the region is plagued by "three key deficits that can be considered defining features":

- a lack of freedom

- disempowerment of women

- a lack of capabilities or knowledge.

THE FATE OF THE PEOPLE

How do people live in this kind of premodern lack of development? The "mass triangle" represents their response. There is also a "power" or "elite triangle," which will be explained in a moment. Reality, of course, is more complex; categories overlap.

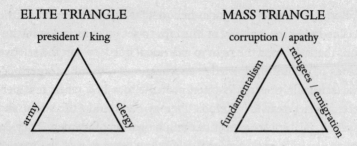

In accordance with tribal culture, the power in the home countries of Muslim immigrants (with the important exception of Turkey) is concentrated in a triangle, consisting of a political leader at the top (either a president or a king), followed by the army, and then the official clergy *('ulema)*. These three sectors (just about) reinforce each other. Its members often come from the same family, clan, or tribe and are related by marriage. Their power is partly based on these relationships. To these people at the top, Islam is an instrument, a means to consolidate the existing balance of power. In states such as Egypt, Iraq, and Syria, the secular government monitors religious leaders, and there is a state religion. The political and army leaders have complete control over the official instruments of force (in the absence of an independent judiciary), all sources of government income (tax and trade), the media (radio, television, newspapers), and the economy. The result is a general stagnation in society.

The mass triangle represents the various ways in which the people respond to this stagnation.

There is corruption and apathy. Only a section of the population has access to public services through the clan or tribe, and these people take advantage of the endemic corruption within the civil service and the business community. A proportion of the financial aid from Western counties and international organizations is taken by this dominant group, which is out to enrich itself and often resorts to bribery and blackmail. The rest of the population tends to accept the situation as it is, because that is all they have ever known.

There is a rise in fundamentalism. This rapidly expanding section of the population does not accept the existing balance of power. Fundamentalists are on the rise everywhere, even among professionals with a high level of education (lawyers, doctors, and others). They are disappointed by secular ideologies such as liberal democracy, nationalism, and communism. Fundamentalists believe that all the social and economic miseries—"What went wrong"—are due to the widespread neglect of Islamic values and standards. The Islamic Brotherhood, Bin Laden's al Qaeda, and Erbakan's Milli Görüs in Turkey accuse the United States, in particular, of supporting tyranny in their countries. In some countries, the fundamentalists are described as the only authentic opposition group in the Islamic world, but of course many countries do also have democratic and/or secular opposition parties. Fundamentalist power depends on zealous missionary work, an antipathy toward government-supported clerics, desperate force (terrorism and martyrdom), and their own religious centers, such as the Al-Azhar University in Egypt.

There is significant internal and external emigration. The biggest victims of social stagnation are rural people, peasants from the countryside. Many have been uprooted and forced to look for work in the cities, where they are condemned to accept low-paid, menial jobs; they often receive a cruel, degrading deal in a society dominated by honor and shame. Often they have little or no education, or are illiterate. Numerous other people who do not have the right tribal or clan background (merchants, tradespeople, low-ranking civil servants, et cetera) are also stuck in poverty.

A small proportion of the peasant masses has been coming to Western Europe as foreign workers since the 1960s. Many left their native countries to escape civil war and famine. A relatively small proportion came to Europe as asylum seekers or to request residence on humanitarian grounds. The large majority—millions—of refugees lives in neighboring countries in Africa and the Mideast, usually in camps managed by the United Nations Human Rights Commission (UNHRC).

The *Arab Human Development Report* states that many in the Islamic world have a very strong desire to emigrate to one of the rich countries in the West.

THE MUSLIM COMMUNITY IN THE NETHERLANDS

The majority of Muslims living in the Netherlands (Turks, Moroccans, and a proportion of asylum seekers) did not make an informed choice to come to the Netherlands, but have ended up there out of necessity. They originally came from the countryside, where tribal traditions still rule.

If we define culture as the repertoire of knowledge, symbols, traditions, ideas, skills, and rules of conduct that make up a community, then the cultural expressions of the majority of Muslims are still at a premodern stage of development. This cultural background is characterized by three important factors. First, an authoritarian mentality based on strict hierarchy; second, a patriarchal family structure, in which the woman has a reproductive function and is expected to obey the men in the family; if she doesn't, she will disgrace the family. Third, all thoughts revolve around the group; the group always comes before the individual; social control is very strong; and the fierce protection of the group's honor makes people obsessed with avoiding shame at all cost, with the result that doing so through lying or simply denying what has really happened becomes the norm. This traditional way of thinking is full of fossilized religious concepts.

It could have been expected that this would lead to big problems with integration at all levels of society, including the workplace. For instance, when a Moroccan warehouse manager of a large supermarket directs his assistants by intimidating and verbally abusing them, he is acting in accordance with the standards of his group (culture). It is his way of establishing authority and defending his honor; management through "positive consultation" would be a sign of weakness. In Moroccan culture you would only begin an instruction with "Would you please . . ." if you were addressing a superior, but not someone of a lower rank than you. The Dutch employees, though, have a different frame of reference; to them the Moroccan's conduct is unworkable and unacceptable. If he refuses to adjust, and to adopt the values of his Dutch staff, he will not be able to function at work and will become unemployed.

Situations like these occur every day. They lead to a great deal of mutual misunderstanding and mistrust, and can result in Muslims complaining of "discrimination" and employers saying that they would rather not employ "any more Moroccans." For a Muslim in the Netherlands, the authoritarian approach is bound to fail. Getting others to agree with you and pursuing your own interests is imbedded in the Dutch social code; it takes into account the individual rights and interests of colleagues. A Muslim newcomer must develop his individual identity outside of his group identity and distance himself from the traditional culture of honor and shame. Instead of seeing himself "through the eyes of others" (honor and shame), he must develop a stable inner compass that will help him survive in a modern Western society.

Another common problem of integration is seen in the relations between men and women. The deeply patriarchal standards of Muslims often seem totally inappropriate, outdated, and degrading in modern society. The virgin/whore cult, the pressure to have as many sons as possible, the circumcision of girls (usually justified on religious grounds), arranged marriages for daughters—these are all products of the mentality of honor. As a group, Muslim women as well as men will have to forgo these practices and their underlying values to succeed in the West. If they do not, the emancipation of Muslims cannot really begin. Or, to put it in the words of the Dutch economist Arie van der Zwan, "this gap between the sealed-off world of non-Western immigrants and the society in which they have arrived cannot be seen separately from the stagnation in their home countries. For most [still] come from the Islamic world, and there is a growing stream of international literature which poses the question of why that world failed: 'What went wrong?' The Islamic world has seen little progress in science, culture, or the economy since the eighteenth century, although it once made major contributions in these areas."

What is particularly good about van der Zwan's statement is that he mentions both the international aspect (stagnation as an impetus for emigration) and the national dimension (cultural problems during integration that present a challenge to the host society). In his article he discusses the factors that have led to both the emigration and the fact that Muslims cling to values and standards that are "unsuitable" in a modern society.

Initially, Dutch politicians and policy makers interpreted the influx of foreign workers from the Muslim world (Morocco and Turkey) as a temporary phenomenon. The newcomers were "guest workers." The Muslims themselves held a similar view, thinking that they had come to the West for a limited time, in order to earn money with which they could build a future back home. As it became clear that Muslims, like other non-Western immigrants, were settling permanently in the Netherlands, the debate about how best to integrate these people into Dutch society began. There are four positions to be distinguished in this debate, which are relevant to all Western democracies.

THE POLITICAL-LEGAL POSITION

In order to become full members of Dutch society, newcomers who possess a residence permit should have the same social and political rights and duties as the native population. Once they meet this political-legal condition, immigrants supposedly can participate in every aspect of society without further government intervention, although the campaign against discrimination and racism remains important to uphold.

The problem with this vision is that there is a gap between immigrants' formal rights and the actual process of settling down and becoming fully emancipated members of society. In practice very few immigrants make use of their civil and political rights. Their turnout at the elections, for example, is depressingly low. Because familiarization with Dutch society is limited, their awareness of their individual rights is, too.

Paradoxically, in practice, formal rights are used to achieve the opposite of integration, namely to segregate the community from the rest of society on the basis of its religion (ethnicity). The most tragic example of this is the government system of subsidies for special Islamic schools. The ease with which immigrants can draw social benefits also has its drawbacks, one of which is that many immigrants have slipped into a permanent dependency on state benefits.

The political-legal approach is based on Dutch national history formed over centuries of political tensions among different Christian and secular groups. It does not take into account the background of the Muslims in the Netherlands. Because there is such a difference between the mind-sets of Muslim immigrants and the Dutch population, however, this approach perpetuates the disadvantages mentioned above. Radical Muslims will not be absorbed into the country the way the Roman Catholics and other sects eventually were in history. Radical Muslims are opposed to the system itself. Radical Muslims want to destroy the whole system.

THE SOCIOECONOMIC ANGLE

In this view, immigrants from non-Western countries are labeled as disadvantaged. The state aims its legislation to create equal opportunities for their education, employment and income, health care, and housing. The group's disadvantages are considered only socioeconomic, however, and are not thought to be byproducts of any culture or religion.

The advantage of this approach is that it takes into consideration the different ways immigrants are excluded, in what we call "blind" segregation. For instance, large numbers of immigrants in deprived areas are virtually segregated into "black" schools, whereas most ethnic Dutch children are in "white" schools. But as before, the disadvantage of this approach is that it is based on the specific circumstances of Dutch social history, in particular the struggle between labor and capital, and the institution of the welfare state after World War II. After this, the Dutch working class became emancipated into a bourgeois middle class. Most Muslims in the Netherlands, on the other hand, come from a completely different background, one of institutionalized inequality, which is why this approach has two major downsides. In the first place, it leads to victimization, because it places all the responsibility for dealing with the problems on external factors (the government, Dutch society); it also gives the group a negative self-image and encourages a distrustful attitude toward the world outside the group. This causes tensions between the parties and gives rise to recriminations.

Moreover, the provisions of the Dutch welfare state, such as social security and rent subsidy, help cushion the consequences for those who have dropped out of society, who no longer absolutely need to adjust to the ways of Dutch society if they want to survive. In this way, the process of modernization comes to a halt for large groups of Muslims; from the margins of society they cling to values and standards that stand in the way of their own emancipation.

MULTICULTURALISM:
INTEGRATION WHILE RETAINING ONE'S OWN IDENTITY

A multicultural approach aspires to promote different cultures living peacefully side by side under one government, in accordance with the rules of mutual respect, and with the same opportunities and rights. Yet advocates of multiculturalism favor giving minorities special privileges. Originally, these special privileges are intended to safeguard the rights of the indigenous population in countries such as Canada (Indians and Inuit) and Australia (Aboriginals). Nonetheless, many people in the Netherlands still defend this position. For example, M. Galenkamp, a philosopher of law from Rotterdam, was critical of the Prime Minister Balkenende's proposal to make the fundamental starting points for the government's integration policy the Dutch system of morals and values (basic human rights) and the separation of church and state. Galenkamp argued that this would be impossible, since the Netherlands is no longer a homogeneous society; she also feels it would have the undesirable effect of polarization, which would be detrimental to social cohesion; and she argues that it would be unnecessary because a better starting point would be the "principle of damage" devised by J. S. Mill, the nineteenth-century philosopher, who believed that no person should ever have to suffer as a result of someone else's exercise of freedom.

If John Stuart Mill were living in Holland today, he would disagree with Galenkamp. He would explain to her that the position of Muslim women living in Holland is already contrary to the "principle of damage." The problem with Galenkamp is that she's very formal in her thinking, as a lawyer is trained to be. Lawyers are not taught to understand the term *power*; they concentrate on the vertical relationships in society—the vertical relationship of the individual and his relationship to the government. So, they argue, the freedom of the individual must not be restricted by the government. But they do not see the way power works horizontally. They do not see how to prohibit one individual from taking the freedom of another individual. They do not see or understand the subcultures, particularly Islamic interior cultures. They do not see how Muslim women are socialized to believe in the importance and rightness of their own oppression. Mill was quite aware of the importance of reading and reasoning as tools of self-understanding and of understanding the world. If a woman is socialized to believe in her own oppression, that would not meet the condition of freedom.

Multiculturalism has been the biggest influence on Dutch integration policies since the realization, around 1979, that the guest workers who had flowed in from other countries to perform service jobs were going to stay for good. Multiculturalism is so influential partly due to the nation's history of having learned to live with many minorities in a peaceful way. This coexistence was based on the principle of "emancipation through the conservation of identity," of the integration of different peoples as they preserved their own ethnic, cultural identities. Multiculturalism is also influential because of the guilt that the Dutch feel over their colonial history and over the racism against and genocide of the Jews during World War II.

The problem with this multicultural view is that it denies that cultural and religious standards can have negative effects and retard the integration and emancipation of peoples, particularly Muslims. Thus, the multiculturalists welcome the emergence of a Muslim section of society because they are under the illusion that it will help encourage Muslim economic emancipation as it did with the Roman Catholic sectors years ago. The Catholics in a largely Protestant Dutch country were for some years poorer, with large families and low-paying jobs, like Muslims today. But they organized themselves around the Catholic Church and improved their financial and economic lives until they became quite integrated.

The multiculturalists say, "If it worked for the Catholics, why shouldn't it work for the Muslims?" But this is a dangerous misconception about the vast majority of Muslims and will merely encourage their separate, inward focus on their own isolated culture. What the multiculturalists forget is that the Catholics shared with the other Christian/Protestant sects the same language, the same national identity, a common history, and basically the same ethnicity. And they were both Christian, although they might disagree on how to express their religion. The Muslims in Europe have myriad different languages and ethnicities that further separate them from their new country. The socioeconomic background of these many peoples is also quite varied and starkly different from the European background. Because multiculturalists will not classify cultural phenomena as "better" or "worse" but only neutral or disparate, they actually encourage segregation and unintentionally perpetuate, for instance, the unsatisfactory position of Muslim women. State subsidies for nonstate schools allow Muslims to have their own schools, including separate boarding schools for boys and girls, in which young girls are indoctrinated to expect a future as mothers and housewives in accordance with very conservative Islamic practices.

THE SOCIOCULTURAL APPROACH

The economist Arie van der Zwan recently concluded that the lack of progress in integration cannot be explained by objective socioeconomic factors alone. Sociocultural factors are equally important and combine with very real socioeconomic disadvantages to cause the integration problem. He draws distinctions, for example, between the various groups of non-Western immigrants. On the one hand, there are the people from Surinam and the Antilles, and on the other the Moroccans and Turks. Referring to the study by the Netherlands Scientific Council of Government Policy, mentioned above, he concludes that the former two groups form a subclass that has become almost identical to its native Dutch counterpart. But Turks and Moroccans present qualitative and quantitative differences, which arise from their sociocultural position. Only a third of the Moroccan and Turkish population can be considered integrated immigrants. For two-thirds, the prospects for integration are very poor indeed.

One-half of the unintegrated group consists of people over forty-five, most of whom have stopped working. The other half consists of second- and third-generation Turks and Moroccans, who, van der Zwan writes, are impossible to classify: "The strong identification with the ethnic group has gone, while integration into society has not taken place yet, and the prospect of this happening is doubtful." This vulnerable, uprooted group is exposed to the temptations of Western society (freedom, drugs, nightlife), but lacks the inner mental or individual resources or education to control inappropriate behavior. Social derailment is common with these young people: education and employment can lead to social elevation, but delinquency and the lure of fundamentalism often are more alluring.

CONCLUSION

If we interpret the concept of "integration" as a process of civilization for groups of Muslim immigrants living *within* the Western society into which they have been received, we render superfluous the pseudodebate about the equality of cultures. Whether an immigrant should accept or give up something in order to function better within a society depends on the demands of that society. As immigrants develop an awareness of their level of achievement in relation to others, they see that in order to progress they need to behave according to the values and standards of their newly adopted home country.

A third advantage of regarding integration as a process of civilization is that it helps the native population to empathize with the immigrants facing this challenge. It is easier to show mutual understanding in the knowledge that the immigrant is about to face a fundamental personal change. The native majority has had over a hundred years to come to grips with modern values, which gives them a psychological advantage over the people who have walked into society straight from the Riff Mountains or the Anatolian countryside. Denying this really would be counterproductive, yet this form of tolerance is quite different from advocating the preservation of traditions and values merely for their own sake.

After all, the Dutch no longer advocate the tradition of an ancestral, premodern, religious tradition. Tragically, however, the Dutch government has ignored the culturally disadvantaged position of Muslims for decades. In recent years, the most common approaches the government took to these problems were the political-legal, the (purely) socioeconomic, and the multicultural, all three of which were strongly colored by typically Dutch political, economic, and cultural traditions. Only an approach that addresses both the socioeconomic disadvantages and cultural factors unique to Islam offers a real chance of promoting successful integration. Failure to do this would be catastrophic, above all for the weakest group of Muslim immigrants, the women and girls.

SIX

A Brief Personal History of My Emancipation

At the time of this interview, I had been forced by death threats to leave the Netherlands to go into hiding. I expected that once I returned to the Netherlands all publicity would—at first—focus on me again and not on the debate. Right now the media are still lapping it up: a black woman who criticizes Islam. One day the magic surrounding me will disappear. At some point they will have had enough, and then it will be possible to think about the real issue again, about the fact that the failure of integration is to a considerable extent due to the hostility toward women in Islamic culture and religion.

I knew what I was letting myself in for when I took this position. The negative reactions did not surprise me. This is a topic that stirs up controversy. If I do go on—and I will—I will have to expect the difficult repercussions that will inevitably follow. I understand that rage. Any group on the brink of a transformation will experience that fury. My strategy is to keep pushing until the storm is over. One day I will be able to say the things I am saying now without inciting these violent emotions. Others have also begun to speak out and are fighting for the emancipation of dependent, semiliterate women from immigrant communities. The third feminist wave is on its way, and it is giving me goose bumps.

Emancipation is a struggle. I chose that struggle and am now going to carry on fighting for it as a member of parliament for the Liberal Party. I decided to switch over to them because I was getting sick of the evasive behavior of the Labor party, which has closed its eyes to the growing feelings of unease in society. Suppression of women does not seem to them to be an important theme, and they are not committed to admitting it occurs, addressing it, or correcting it.

I have not chosen to join the Liberal Party, not because I care less about social issues on which the Labor Party thinks it has a monopoly, but because I have come to realize that social justice begins with the freedom and integrity of the individual. Everything in our society focuses on the individual citizen: you take your exams on your own, you fill in your own tax form, and in court you alone have to face your sentence. Personal responsibility always comes first. But what does the Labor Party do? It still treats immigrants as a group. You might ask yourself, why? The answer is, because this party is not in touch with reality.

Let me give an example. As an interpreter I was involved with immigrants who had committed social security fraud. In order to claim an allowance, both partners have to sign; the woman does this at her husband's command. He points to the dotted line and says "sign here." But she has no idea what she is signing for. In her home country she has never had to do anything like this. Then the police come to the door. The man and woman are charged with social security fraud. It turns out that the husband had a job on the side. She, however, knew nothing about it: true, he leaves the house every morning and comes home late at night, but Muslim men rarely tell their wives how they spend the day. So why should she have noticed anything? It emerges that they have to pay back eighty thousand guilders, half each. In other words, the wife is made jointly responsible for the husband's misconduct. And this case is by no means unique; there are hundreds like it.

Try to convince the Labor Party that these women should be freed from their dependent position; you won't succeed. The party aims to keep Muslim women in this position because it thinks that it will help the women's sense of identity. "Those women," they say, "are happy in their own culture." The party overlooks the children, too. Until, that is, they turn into little "Moroccan bastards." Then there is the devil to pay.

In a Dutch newsmagazine, a general practitioner and well-known member of the Labor Party relates how a Muslim woman came to his surgery and said: "It is God's will that my husband has become so ill." The thought that your life lies in the hands of God may offer you comfort on your deathbed, but it also means that you will end up sooner on that deathbed. However, this doctor thinks it is a "nice conviction." As it happens, he does not believe in God himself, but it seems agreeable to him to be able to utter this kind of nonsense. What he is actually saying is: they have a right to their own backwardness.

The deciding factor for my changeover in October 2002 to the Liberal Party was the assurance by the party leader that I will be given the freedom to bring to the top of the political agenda the integration and emancipation of immigrant women.

I do not understand why my decision has generated such an emotional response. People use words like *treason,* as if I had joined a criminal organization. But after eight years of a coalition government composed of the Liberal and Labor parties, the differences between the two parties are really not that big. I can understand that people feel let down by me personally. However, the fact that Labor has done a lot for me does not mean I should remain loyal to the party when I can no longer identify with its viewpoints. Everyone suggests it was an impulsive decision, but I had already said back in August that I was not happy and wanted to leave.

Of course, I have to learn certain things. I understand that at times I must strike a compromise, that I need to become more strategic in my thinking and formulate my thoughts more accurately, but I have no intention of giving up. I can live with the price I have to pay for this. As long as I am protected, I have the mental energy to go on. I need to be careful, though, not to push for too much too fast. My impatience is my Achilles' heel: I want it all to happen here and now. I need to be told that tomorrow will still be good.

I KNOW MY father loves me, but I have made a choice that radically opposes everything he stands for. If he really said to the Dutch weekly what he is quoted as saying—that he never received any phone threats—it feels to me like a slap in the face. After each of my public appearances he received telephone calls from Somali Muslims who wanted to lodge a complaint. Initially he ignored these calls, but he did ask me whether the stories were true. I told him that I was making a stand for the rights of women in Islam. His reaction was: "Make a stand for what you feel is right, but make sure you do it in God's name." The fact that I have now publicly denounced God is a terrible disappointment to him, one he can barely accept. By smearing Islam, I have smeared his reputation and his honor. That is why he has turned away from me. I feel for him, but at the same time I am furious. At the end of the book that I am writing at the moment, I address an open letter to him in which I accuse him of offering his children conditional love only. Every time he has had to make a choice between the community and his children, he has chosen the former. This hurts.

I am a real daddy's girl. During the short periods he spent with our family, he was wonderfully kind to me and praised me to the skies. He also organized some things for which I feel indebted to him to this day. For example, when we were living in Ethiopia my mother did not want my sister or me to attend school. We were going to be married off within a few years anyway, so what good would all that knowledge be to us? We were better off learning to do the housework. But my father insisted that we go to school. He said he would curse my mother forever if she would not let us. He also declared himself dead set against our circumcision. What he doesn't know is that my grandmother secretly arranged to have it done behind his back.

My brother, my sister, and I did tackle him about never spending any time with us. He had brought us into the world but took no responsibility for it. We had nothing against his political activities, felt quite proud even, but we also wanted a father. He thought our criticisms were unworthy of us. Trivial moaning. We should see that he had a vocation and therefore make sacrifices with our heads up. God had bestowed the honor of this position upon him.

When I was born my father was in prison. I was six years old when I first saw him. Even though our father was absent for long periods, as children we sensed the tension surrounding his political activities. I always refer to the years in Somalia as the *whispering years*. Hush, hush, nobody can be trusted. I can remember hearing the pounding on the door, my grandmother opening it and being tossed to the floor, the verbal abuse of men ransacking our house. A child cannot understand these things.

On my sixth birthday we followed my father—who had by then fled the country—to Saudi Arabia. None of us felt happy there, with the exception of my mother, who flourished in a country with such a strict religious climate. But she also compared the local inhabitants to goats and sheep because she found them so stupid. We had to wear a green, long-sleeved dress to school and tightly wrap a scarf around our heads. The heat gave us blisters on our backs. We were not allowed to play outside. After a year we moved to Ethiopia, where a large part of the Somali opposition lived, and then, after eighteen months, to Kenya.

My father has five daughters and a son, by four different wives. My mother was his second wife. He met her when his first wife, Maryan, was in America. She had been sent there by him to study, but she didn't do very well. My father wanted her to stay away until she managed to get her diplomas. Meanwhile, at home, he had become one of the organizing forces behind the campaign for literacy. He was a teacher himself and my mother was his pupil. He thought she was smart and ambitious, and married her. Within a short period they had three children, and then one day Maryan turned up at the door, back from America. She knew nothing about his second marriage and was furious. She demanded that he make a choice. My father chose my mother and divorced Maryan.

In 1980 he left for Ethiopia. After a year he came back to visit us. My mother said, "If you leave again now, I don't want you to come back ever again, and I will no longer be your wife." He went away and returned after ten years. My mother refused to greet him and has stuck to this to the present day. Later he married an Ethiopian woman, and then someone from Somalia—I have no idea where they are now. Eventually he remarried Maryan, his first wife, with whom he lives in London.

Besides an older brother, I had a sister, Haweya, who was two years younger than I and for whom I felt strong admiration. Haweya was rebellious. She did what she wanted, and she didn't care if she received a beating for it. I was more timid and docile, tending to accept things as they were. But she never did. As a teenager Haweya wanted to wear short skirts, something that was considered thoroughly indecent. My mother ripped them up, but each time she did, my sister just bought herself a new one. During her second year in high school she quit. Everyone was furious, but she couldn't have cared less. She successfully completed a secretarial course and found a job at the United Nations. My mother forbade her to work, but my sister defied her, despite verbal and physical abuse.

Haweya was a strong woman and commanded admiration and respect everywhere except at home. When her turn came to be married off, she followed me to the Netherlands. She arrived in January 1994, and after a year and a half her Dutch was good enough to enroll at university. But she started to become tearful and her behavior became eccentric. She struggled in the company of others but could not manage being on her own either. She watched television for hours on end, regardless of what was on. She would lie in bed for days and didn't eat. After a time she revealed that she was unhappy because she had neglected her faith. She began to wear a headscarf and tried to pray. Some days she could not manage it and that increased her feelings of guilt, because for every prayer you miss, there is a punishment. She also kept saying, I am suffering so much, but nobody understands me. And she was ashamed of the way she had behaved toward my mother in the past and deeply regretted all those arguments.

Then one day Haweya had a mental breakdown and had to go into hospital. She was treated with medication to which she responded well, though she did suffer some side effects: restlessness, pain, stiff muscles, strange twitches. I saw my sister, that beautiful, strong woman, cracking up before my eyes.

In July 1997, Haweya returned to Kenya. Instead of medication she received visits from mullahs who had been summoned to drive out her psychoses. They commanded her to read the Koran so that she would calm down. And she was dragged to an exorcist because some people thought that my stepmother had bewitched her. My sister said to the exorcist, If you are capable of releasing such extraordinary powers, you should use them to heal your rotten teeth. In her madness she never lost her wit. Occasionally they tied her up or beat her in order to calm her down, but of course that solved nothing. The manic attacks just grew more uncontrollable. She suffered paranoia and stopped eating. On January 8, 1998, she died.

Haweya's death was the hardest moment of my life. When my father gave me the news over the telephone, I burst into tears, at which he said, "Why are you so upset? You know we all return to God." I jumped on the first plane to Nairobi but arrived too late for the funeral. Presumably she died from exhaustion, but I will never be sure because no autopsy was performed. In our culture it is taboo to ask questions about the cause of death. Every time I brought up the subject, I was dismissed as a tiresome child who keeps asking the same old question. The response was invariably: God gives and takes life away.

My sister and I were still very young when we began to notice that we were always told to respect our brother. He was only ten months older than I, but we realized that only boys count. A Muslim woman's status depends on the number of sons she has. When people asked my grandmother how many children she had, she would answer: "One." She had nine daughters and a son. She was the same with regard to our family, said we had only one child. "What about us?" Haweya and I would ask. "You are going to bear sons for us," she replied. It drove me to desperation. What was I to do with my life on earth? Bear sons! Become a production plant for sons. I was nine years old at the time.

To maximize their potential as producers of sons, girls are taught from early on always to conform—to God, to their father and brothers, to the family, to the clan. The better a woman seems at this, the more virtuous she is thought to be. You should always be patient, even when your husband demands the most dreadful things of you. You will be rewarded for this in the hereafter. But the reward itself is small. Women can look forward to dates and grapes in paradise. That is all.

When we were living in Saudi Arabia, my brother was always allowed to go everywhere with my father. We had to stay at home. But my sister and I were inquisitive children. We wanted to come, too, thought it was unfair. That was a word that touched a chord in my father. We knew this. And he immediately wanted to set the record straight. "Allah has said: 'I have given woman an honorable position. I have placed paradise underneath her feet.'" We looked down at my mother's feet, and then at my father's, and burst out laughing. As always, his were covered by expensive leather shoes from Italy, while my mother's were bare, the skin badly cracked and peeling from walking on cheap sandals. My father laughed with us, but my mother grew angry, hit us, and sent us out of the room. She was terrified of blasphemy.

In Kenya I went from my primary school to the Muslim Girls Secondary School. The school was attended by girls from Kenya but also from Yemen, Somalia, Pakistan, and India. There were some very bright girls there, who were good at everything, academic subjects as well as sport. In the mornings our names were called out. You had to say "Present." But after a certain age there seemed to be a growing number of absent girls. No one knew where they had gone. Later we heard that they had been married off. Some I met again after a year or two. There was nothing left of them. All those girls had become production plants for sons: plump, pregnant, or already holding a child in one arm. The fighting spirit, the light in their eyes, the jittery energy had all vanished. Among these girls, suicide and depression were common. In a way I was lucky that my father was not living with us at the time. Otherwise I would probably also have been contracted to marry someone when I was sixteen, and at that age you cannot run away. Where could I have fled?

From the mid-1980s Islam was becoming more prominent in Kenya. Like many other adolescents I was looking for something, and I was strongly impressed by our Islam teacher. She looked striking, with a pale, heart-shaped face that formed a mysterious contrast with her black headscarf and long black dress. She could talk passionately about the love of God and our duties to Him. It was through her teaching that I first felt the need to become a martyr. It would bring me closer to God. Submission to Allah's will—that was what it was about. We repeated this sentence over and over, like a mantra: "We subject ourselves to God's will." I spontaneously began to wear a veil and black garments over my school uniform. My mother was thrilled, my sister less so.

Then I got a boyfriend. That was forbidden. We kissed. That was worse than forbidden. On top of everything he was a very religious boyfriend, strict when it came to doctrines regarding the relations between men and women. But in actual life he did not observe the rules. At that moment I experienced my first strong doubts. Because I lied and he lied. The more religious I became, the more I found myself lying and deceiving. That seemed wrong.

Later on I stayed in a refugee camp on the border between Somalia and Kenya. I saw how women who had been raped during the war were abandoned. And I asked myself, If God exists, why does He allow this? It was forbidden to think such thoughts, let alone speak them, but my belief was crumbling. Nonetheless I continued to call myself a Muslim.

September 11 was a decisive turning point, but it was not until six months later, after I had read *The Atheist Manifesto* by Herman Philipse, that I dared to admit to others that I no longer believed. I had been given the book in 1998 by my boyfriend Marco but didn't want to read it at the time. I thought: an atheist manifesto is a declaration of the devil. I could feel an inner resistance. But recently I felt ready. The time had come. I saw that God was an invention and that subjection to His will meant nothing more than subjecting yourself to the willpower of the strongest.

I have nothing against religion as a source of comfort. Rituals and prayers can provide support, and I am not asking anyone to give those up. But I do reject religion as a moral gauge, a guideline for life. And this applies above all to Islam, which is an all-pervasive religion, dominating every step of your life.

People blame me for not drawing a distinction between religion and culture. Female circumcision, they say, has nothing to do with Islam, because this cruel ritual does not take place in all Islamic societies. But Islam demands that you enter marriage as a virgin. The virginity dogma is safeguarded by locking girls up in their homes and sewing their outer labia together. Female circumcision serves two purposes: the clitoris is removed in order to reduce the woman's sexuality, and the labia are sewn up in order to guarantee her virginity.

Circumcision dates back to pre-Islamic times, when the ritual was observed among certain animist tribes. Clans in Kenya first circumcised their women out of a fear that the clitoris would grow too large during child delivery and smother the baby. But these existing local practices were spread by Islam. They became more important and were sanctified. In countries such as Sudan, Egypt, and Somalia, where Islam is a big influence, the emphasis on virginity is very strong.

People also say that my negative image of Islam is the product of personal trauma. I am not saying that I had a rosy childhood, but I managed to get through it. It would be selfish to keep my experiences and insights to myself. It wouldn't be feasible. Young Muslim girls in the Netherlands who still have the light in their eyes do not have to go through what I did. We must face the facts and offer to immigrants what they are denied in their own culture: individual dignity. The big obstacle to the integration of immigrants is undeniably Islam.

Marco—my former boyfriend who gave me *The Atheist Manifesto*—lived in the same students' house as I did. We circled around each other for two months and then we fell in love. I didn't mention it to my parents. But I told my brother, who demanded that I break off the relationship immediately. I ignored him. Marco and I lived together for five years. Incidentally, it was a big step for me to move in with someone else. That went right into the teeth of what is conventionally expected in our culture: you remain a virgin until you are married off. In the end it did not work out because we are both strong-willed and neither of us is inclined to give in. That always led to arguments. Moreover, I am rather scattered, while he is meticulous and strict. That also gave rise to problems. We are still very fond of each other; it just became impossible to go on. Around us we saw other relationships trying to survive despite tremendous pressure, with all its consequences. We did not want that.

The fact that I did not want to be married—not to a distant cousin in Canada nor to anyone else—could not be discussed. My father said: "Child, just trust me to know what is best for you." But I did not trust him, and I fled to the Netherlands. I wrote him what I think was a loving but unambiguous letter, in which I begged him to let me have my freedom. He sent it back to me. In the margin he had written in red ink that he regarded this as an act of treason, that he never wanted to see me again, and that I was no longer to call myself his child. We did not speak for six years. One evening in 1997 the phone rang. Marco answered, listened, and handed me the receiver. "I think it's your father," he said. I took the receiver and heard "Abbe," my child. He had forgiven me and wanted to let me know he was proud of me because I was taking good care of my sister. I wept and wept. It was one of the most beautiful days in my life. He had taken me back as his daughter.

SEVEN

Being a Politician
Is Not My Ideal

1. Thou shalt have no other gods before me.

My faith has been a faith of fear. Fear of making mistakes. Fear of incurring Allah's anger. Fear of being sent to hell; fear of flames and of fire. Allah was like the government: always present, everywhere; ready to arrest my father and lock him away in prison. My relationship with Allah was like this: as long as He left me in peace, I was happy. Certainly, I prayed when I was in pain; I begged Him to stop my mother from beating me. But like any child who, sooner or later, realizes at the back of his mind that Santa Claus does not exist, I accepted that I should not expect much from Him.

I think I am an atheist at heart; it just took me a while to find my convictions confirmed in print somewhere. This may sound arrogant, but I think that most people who call themselves religious are essentially atheists. They avoid thinking about whether they really believe in God and allow themselves to be distracted by details. We should have a debate in the Netherlands about the source of our moral standards: did we people invent them, or were they the work of God? We should begin by analyzing the things our prime minister—or any world leader—says. Have you ever listened to him properly? He is forever referring to biblical standards and values, never to the things God asks us to do or forbids us. Yet he is an academic, a man who has learned to use well-reasoned arguments to find certain truths. Can he believe that the world was created in six days? That Eve was created from Adam's rib? That simply cannot be true. Scientists are unbelieving. I am convinced that our prime minister is not a Christian.

2. Thou shalt not make unto thee any graven image,
or any likeness of any thing that is in heaven above, or
that is in the earth beneath, or that is in the water
under the earth.

With the first commandment Muhammad wanted to lock away common sense, and with the second he subjugated the beautiful, romantic side of mankind. I am really appalled that so many people are denied access to art. In this respect, Islam is a culture that has been outlived, by which I mean it is an unchanging, fossilized culture. Everything is written down in the Koran, and that is the end of the discussion. Personally, I still find the teachings of Muhammad outdated, but since in my present capacity as politician I can't afford to enter into an argument with people who will forever accuse me of having called them backward, I had to take back that remark. Or, rather, I modified my statement: I find the principle of Islam—to submit yourself to Allah's will—a backward point of departure, but that doesn't mean that I find those who adhere to the belief primitive as well. They are behind in their development, which is not the same thing. It is not too late to make progress.

3. Thou shalt not take the name of the Lord thy God in vain.

It is a capital offense to insult God's prophet, Muhammad. God himself let this be known to the Prophet, as He gave him other such opportune messages. You need only read the Koran: He stole Zayneb, His pupil's wife, with the excuse that it was Allah's will. And, even worse: he fell in love with Aisha, his best friend's nine-year-old daughter. Her father said: "Please wait until she has reached adulthood." But Muhammad did not want to wait. So what do you think happens? He receives a message from Allah that Aisha must prepare herself for Muhammad. In other words, Muhammad teaches us that it is fine to take away your best friend's child. By our Western standards Muhammad is a perverse man. A tyrant. He is against freedom of expression. If you don't do as he says, you will end up in hell. That reminds me of those megalomaniacal rulers in the Middle East: Bin Laden, Khomeini, and Saddam. Are you surprised to find a Saddam Hussein? Muhammad is his example; Muhammad is an example to all Muslim men. Why do you think so many Islamic men use violence? You are shocked to hear me say these things, but like the majority of the native Dutch population, you overlook something: you forget where I am from. I used to be a Muslim; I know what I am talking about. I think it is tragic that, now that I finally live in a democratic society, where freedom of opinion is the greatest good, I still have to struggle with the posthumous blackmail of the Prophet Muhammad. In the Netherlands a Muslim can read the Koran and think that Muhammad is fantastic. And I am also allowed to think that Muhammad is a despicable individual. He says women should stay indoors, wear a veil, avoid certain types of work, can't have the same rights of inheritance as their husbands, and should be stoned if they commit adultery. I want to show that there is another reality, besides the "truth," which is spread across the world with Saudi money. I realize that the women who call themselves Muslims do not understand me yet, but one day their blinkers will drop. We must open up all the channels of socialization—family, education, the media—to make sure that Muslim women become independent and self-supporting. This will take many years, but one day these women will realize, as I did: I don't want my mother's life.

4. Remember the Sabbath day, to keep it holy. Six days shalt thou labor, and do all thy work: but the seventh day is the Sabbath of the Lord, thy God: in it thou shalt not do any work.

At busy times I think, Now I must recover myself. At such moments I like to be by myself for a bit. Walk around in pajamas, read a book, or just stay in bed. Yes, hanging around, that's what it amounts to. There was a time when I would sit around like this for three days in a row, but in recent months that hasn't happened. I think the Christian use of Sundays will stand me in good stead.

5. Honor thy father and mother.

Allah says, First you must obey me, then the Prophet Muhammad, and finally your father and mother. Obey them in everything. There is only one moment when you are allowed to refuse them: when they ask you to stop believing in Allah. I waited a long time before I openly declared my break with Islam. I was afraid of the consequences, of losing my family. All my life I had been sitting on the fence until I couldn't any longer. Everything I do now, the things I write and say, I could not have done if I had remained in that awkward position. Now there is a big empty god between my family and me; they no longer wish to see me. That is how perverse religion can be: it interferes with intimate relationships and forces parents to choose between their children and their god.

They are always in my thoughts. I miss them. There is sadness. And yet I am better able to control my guilty feelings now that I no longer believe I will have to pay for my disobedience with a place in hell. What makes me particularly sad is the thought that it is all so unnecessary: why don't they accept me as I am? I want my father to be there when I am sworn into the Dutch Lower House of Parliament. I want him to hold and cuddle me, like he used to. It won't happen. I want to send my mother money, but the money won't reach her. I want to know how she is, but I am afraid to phone her. She has chosen Allah, not me.

My mother is a strict woman with a strong will. She knows how to manipulate her surroundings, and if it doesn't work, she hits you and starts throwing things about. Everything in our house used to be broken. She was cool, distant, a perfectionist. If I managed to give nine out of ten correct answers at school, all she would ask was why I had got one wrong. I was afraid of her, but I also admired her. She was always there for us, and she had to do it all on her own. My father was the most important man in Somalia when he first met my mother. That was shortly after the country became independent. My father was busy with politics twenty-four hours a day, setting up a parliament and a literacy program. When the democratic movement failed and my father ended up in prison, she was very loyal to him. She went to visit him every day, often taking him food. But when she was tired and needed his support, he wasn't there for her. This happened again and again. We had to follow him to different countries, where people spoke languages that she—the proud daughter of a prominent judge—couldn't understand; where she had to leave the house—although Allah had asked her to stay inside—in order to converse, in poor Arabic, with the local shopkeepers. I can understand why she became so bitter. It is not a fair comparison, but I can't deny it: I miss my father more than my mother. He was affectionate, cuddled us, and played with us. My father used to say I was beautiful. And smart. He would praise me very highly. When my father was with us I was happy. But he kept leaving us without saying good-bye properly. The last time he left the house, he said "I'll be back next weekend," but we didn't see him again until ten years later. And yet . . . yes, perhaps our loss of contact is the heaviest price I have had to pay. I want to go and visit him, but I know he will shut the door in my face. I know he prefers to remain under the illusion that I am mentally ill. But I will keep trying. When I miss him, when I feel the urge to speak to him, when I would like him to give me a hug, the way he used to, I am enough of a realist to know that he won't listen to me this time. But I am also enough of an idealist to keep hoping that one day he will answer the door again.

6. Thou shalt not kill.

There are a few religious fanatics around who will want to kill me because I have become an atheist, and because—by killing me— they will secure a place in heaven for themselves. Or so they believe. But I think that I pose a threat, above all, to those Muslims who fear that I might be able to influence Dutch opinion, and thus see to it that subsidies to ethnic minorities will be withdrawn and Islamic schools closed. Don't forget: I already have many Dutch Muslims on my side, but they are keeping it under tight cover. As soon as they reveal themselves, as soon as things begin to change and new laws become accepted, the drive to kill me will cease. To me it is simply a matter of persevering. How much longer will I need protection? Not very long. This is not just about me. Islam and the way in which people or parties devote themselves to defending Muhammad's doctrines have become a topic for international debate, documented in United Nations reports. Bin Laden and his followers have achieved exactly the opposite of what they had in mind. Things will probably have to get worse first—the United States' invasion of Iraq will show how much worse—but September 11, mark my words, was the beginning of the end of Islam as we know it.

7. Thou shalt not commit adultery.

I was contracted to marry a distant cousin and start a family with him in Canada. When I ran off, my father disowned me. With the passage of time my father regretted his decision and went to great lengths to get me a divorce. He felt I should marry again; the prospect of me staying childless was unbearable to him. Last summer the divorce was settled, but of course the good news fades once you know I was never faithful to my husband in those years. I have had various boyfriends and lived with someone for five years. I never told my father, but the Somali community in the Netherlands—which keeps close tabs on me—undoubtedly passed on the information. It's not looking good for me: for committing lechery I should be given ten strokes of the cane, according to the Koran, and for committing adultery I could be stoned.

Outside the religious context I have always been loyal. I have observed that people find it difficult to enter a relationship with me. Marco, the boy with whom I lived for a while, used to say I was elusive. "You don't express yourself," he would say. "I never know where I stand with you." It is true that I find it hard to attach myself to others, but I do it all the same. (It is more likely that I will break up with someone because of an argument.) I am on good terms with Marco now; so good, in fact, that he is wondering why we don't move in together again. But I know how quickly he flies off the handle, and I just don't want to have to go through that again. I am not good at expressing my anger. I don't want to; I come from a family whose members were always squabbling, and now I want the opposite.

8. *Thou shalt not steal.*

My mother thought exercise classes were indecent. She refused to give me the extra money required by the school, so I stole it. I did the same in order to attend singing lessons and to buy the crayons we needed for school. As soon as she noticed money had gone missing from her purse, she would begin to swear, grab me by the hair, and pull me all the way across the room. I was always covered in bruises. She struck me with her hand, a stick, or anything she could lay her hands on. I also used to steal food from my mother's pantry to give to the beggars passing our door. The first time this happened, my mother seemed mildly amused, but when she saw a whole crowd waiting outside the house one day—and realized our food for the entire month had vanished from the cupboard—she flew into a rage.

A saint? Me? Not by a long stretch. I have sinned according to the religious principles I was brought up to observe. I've also been naughty—teased other girls at school, rung people's bells and run away, hurt my grandmother's feelings by questioning her authority. And if that is not bad enough, let me tell you how I was responsible for stigmatizing our Koran teacher. When my mother came to the conclusion that sending us to Koran school was a waste of time, she hired a private teacher to teach us at home. We had to prepare our own ink and copy out passages from the Koran on wooden boards. Then we had to wash the boards and start all over again. Every Saturday. After a while I got fed up and locked myself in the lavatory, together with my sister. The teacher, my mother, or my grandmother—whoever it was that came to the door—we refused to open it. I shouted the most dreadful things at the Koran teacher, that writing on boards was obsolete, even back in the sixteenth century. At a certain point my mother sent the teacher away: "Here is your money, they don't want to have Koran lessons. I'm exhausted, I'm giving up." Not much later—I was at home on my own—I saw the Koran teacher approaching our house. I ran to the gate, but it was too late. He dragged me into the house, blindfolded me, and began to hit me. He thumped me, again and again, until I managed to pull off the blindfold. Then he took hold of my head and threw me against the wall. More than once. I heard a crack and lost consciousness. It turned out he had fractured the base of my skull. I had to stay in hospital for twelve days and the bill was sent to him. On top of that, he had to pay us compensation for the grief he had caused. After that he couldn't show himself anywhere. Damaged for life. I will have to live with that: I drove someone to destruction.

9. *Thou shalt not bear false witness against thy neighbor.*

I mastered the art of lying. But when I no longer needed to lie—there is no God; I don't have to tell the truth just because God wants me to—I made a conscious choice never to do so again.

10. *Thou shalt not covet thy neighbor's house, thou shalt not covet thy neighbor's wife, nor his manservant, nor his maidservant, nor his ox, nor his ass, nor anything that is thy neighbor's.*

It depends on what you covet. I would like to write philosophic treatises, like Karl Popper, for example. So, paradoxically, this step—going into politics—is not in line with my ideal. What I would like to do best is become a philosopher and develop my own theories. A place where I can write; someone to do the cleaning; no worries about bread and butter; real debates instead of pointless talk about nothing. Ultimately, that is what will make me happy.

EIGHT

Bin Laden's Nightmare

Interview with Irshad Manji

At the age of fourteen the Ugandan-born Canadian writer Irshad Manji was expelled from school for asking critical questions about Islam. But she was undaunted. She continued to study her religion by herself from her room at home. Thus she became, in the eyes of many Muslims, a traitor. For Irshad Manji is a harsh critic of Islam in newspaper articles, books, and lectures. And she openly admits to being a lesbian.

To mark the publication of the Dutch translation of Manji's *The Trouble with Islam,* I met with her for an interview.

I notice that in your book you address your "fellow Muslims." Do you still consider yourself a Muslim?

Yes, I am a Muslim. I want to be one, because I'm convinced that we can reform Islam. Believe me, when I was expelled from school I learned more about Islam on my own than could be learned by all those Muslims on the other side of the school walls. If only more Muslims would do the same—think for themselves, that is—our religion would be very different. I have noticed that many young Muslims are keen to. Whenever I give a talk at a university, students come up to me afterward and say, "Help, we are suffocating; this religion is strangling us." That is why I wrote the book.

But do you feel you are a Muslim because it's part of your identity, or is it just that you happened to grow up within the system?

No, it's not about identity. What I care about are human rights. I can't keep quiet when I see women who are suffering humiliation in the name of Islam. I constantly urge my fellow Muslims: stop being so selfish. Get up and say something! Women who choose to wear headscarves and face veils always point out to me that it is up to them whether they do or don't. To which I say, Yes, it is fine for you: you have the choice to wear these garments. But think of your sisters who are living under a tough regime that forces them to wear headscarves and will oppress and abuse them if they don't. Fight for them. The Prophet Muhammad himself said: religion is the way in which we behave toward others. In other words, if you brush your responsibilities under the carpet, you have no right to call yourself a Muslim.

But Muhammad also married a nine-year-old girl. Don't you think that's awful?

Of course I do. I don't know Muhammad, I never met him. I can't prove he was a feminist, or a misogynist, for that matter. But the Koran contains a number of very modern-sounding statements by him. I always make a point of asking Muslim men: why is it that you have a beard and dress in seventeenth-century Arabian costume, but you won't take an interest in any of the progressive ideas which Muhammad also included in the Koran?

In theory, Islam is a beautiful and tolerant religion. The problem, however, is that this beautiful religion is weighed down with the pressures of Arabian cultural imperialism, which dictate that women must give up their individuality in honor of the family and become communal property. A raped girl is given one hundred eighty lashes with the whip because she had sex before marriage. We must rid ourselves of such practices.

Yet that remains very difficult. Islam has its roots in Arabian cultural heritage. Before A.D. 610, when a man in a cave suddenly had a few ideas, Islam didn't exist.

And that is precisely why any reform of Islam is so hard. Independent thinking is not encouraged in Arabian culture. Yet it is the only chance Islam has. To get millions of Muslims to think for themselves, no, that is not going to happen. But we can try to form a strong, critical voice, which will prevail upon the rest. The important thing is that we don't allow a small group of mullahs to tell us what to do, but that we Western Muslims—for that is the group I have pinned my hopes on—will have the courage to discover for ourselves how ambiguous and contradictory the Koran is, and to discuss our findings freely.

How do you get Western Muslims to do this?

We need politicians who have the courage to say these things, who aren't afraid of being called controversial and racist. Just like you can't interpret everything in the Koran literally, the multicultural society should not be seen as a dogma. The thing to remember is that people, whether they are Muslims or not, only have the right to be respected if they themselves respect others. You can't deal with human rights and apply double standards.

Why are liberal, secular Westerners so afraid of taking a stance against the abuses of Islam?

You tell me! I have been asking myself that question for a very long time. What are you so anxious about? I ask my friends in the West. Why do you not condemn the violation of human rights in Islamic countries, when you regularly speak out against such atrocities in the United States and Israel?

In the Netherlands, Muslims claim they are demonized by the press, which drives them into the arms of terrorism.

Nobody is forced by journalists to do anything they don't want. Does your head belong to someone else rather than to you? Everything you do here in the free West is *your* choice. For heaven's sake, grow up! Take responsibility for yourself. That is the crux of the matter with the Muslims; they have never been good at taking responsibility for themselves. At the madrassas [Koran lessons] we have it hammered into us that Islam is superior. Historically, the Koran was conceived after the Jewish Torah, and therefore it is thought to contain God's final word. This is a dangerous viewpoint because it condones anything that is done in the name of Islam, even if it seems wrong. No Muslim, not even a well-educated and moderate one, can safely raise any issues related to his faith. Simply and solely because we have never learned to ask a single question about the Koran.

Muslims in the Netherlands are quick to accuse anyone critical of Islam of racism.

I find this terribly hypocritical. The kind of racism Muslims have to put up with in the West is nothing compared to the treatment non-Arabs in the Arabian world suffer. Nobody here is putting the slightest obstacle in the way of the Muslims. On the contrary: people are careful not to take too firm a line against female circumcision because that is part of "their culture." Surely, culture is not a reason to tolerate human suffering. Why are the police not allowed to intervene when a father threatens to kill his daughter if she does not want to be circumcised? The standard reply is that Western women are just as much manipulated by the ideals of beauty that dominate their culture. They feel under pressure to have plastic surgery. But there is a big difference: I have never heard of a situation in which parents disowned their daughter because she refused to have her breasts enlarged. But I am aware of such cases if the daughter did not want to be circumcised or enter into an arranged marriage. The worst thing is that this worry about discrimination pushes Muslim women even further down into the pit. Whom do you help by saying nothing? It's selfish not to want to appear racist.

I read somewhere on the Web that you have been dubbed Bin Laden's nightmare.

I am openly lesbian. Muslims are forced to regard this as a sin. We have held this view for hundreds of years, they say. Is that a valid argument for rejecting homosexuals? Because you have been doing it for such a long time? The Koran states that the diversity of nature is a blessing. That should shut them up.

NINE

Freedom Requires Constant Vigilance

At times I end up in an unfamiliar situation that will lead me in a new direction. This has happened a few times recently. I became a politician, for instance; and, stranger still, I joined the conservative liberal VVD Party [People's Party for Freedom and Democracy]. Now, who would have expected that? Certainly not me.

In 2002, I was having lunch in at a restaurant in the basement of the Dutch house of representatives. Here journalists can have a drink with politicians in a relaxed atmosphere and ask them questions off the record. As I was sitting there, a nice, charming gentleman came up to my table and asked if I would be willing to say a few words on May 4 (Memorial Day in memory of World War II victims) about freedom of speech.

The charming gentleman in question was Caspar Becx, the newly appointed chairman of the Nieuwspoort International Press Centre. He said he found it strange that I had been threatened in the Netherlands as a consequence of using my right to say what I think. Is it not strange to be a member of parliament and not to be able to go anywhere without bodyguards?

He has a point, I thought. And so, on the spur of the moment, I agreed to Mr. Becx's request.

It was not until later, when I was preparing my speech, that I realized I had to say something on the occasion of May 4, Memorial Day, the most politically sensitive and emotional day in the year. Memorial Day is a symbol of the most gruesome period in Dutch and European history. In the Netherlands alone, 240,000 people were killed, among them more than 100,000 Jews. What had I let myself in for when I said yes? What could I, born in Somalia and having lived scarcely ten years in the Netherlands, possibly contribute to such an important and serious day? Could Mr. Becx not have found someone else to do justice to the symbolism of May 4? A member of the Resistance, for example? Or perhaps a relative of such a person? After all, some 25,000 people were actively involved in the Dutch resistance movement during World War II. The fact that I do my work as a member of parliament surrounded by bodyguards does not really warrant my making a speech in defense of freedom of speech. About 1,200 illegal news pamphlets were published during the war; there are people in the Netherlands who put their lives at risk to produce and circulate these pamphlets. Without the added luxury of bodyguards. Why had they not been invited to say something?

TODAY IS MAY 4, and I find myself in the peculiar situation in which you, dear guests, expect me to make a meaningful speech. But what can an immigrant add to May 4 [Memorial Day] or May 5 [Liberation Day]? Do I share the collective memory of the Dutch or, for that matter, the European war generation? And why should I commemorate their dead, when in my own country and continent of origin, there are countless people who die every day and will be completely forgotten.

But perhaps, on second thought, the idea to invite an immigrant to speak today is not that strange after all. The war ended fifty-eight years ago, and the majority of the Dutch population feels that it is genuinely a thing of the past. Formally the country has made its peace with Germany. The younger, postwar generations are feeling increasingly far removed from it. Freedom, and freedom of speech, have become a common experience in the Netherlands. In present-day Europe words can still have a strong impact. They touch, hurt, and offend people. But rarely does this lead to prosecution or threats. We undervalue freedom of speech. Maybe we shouldn't always take it for granted.

Many immigrants have experienced extreme pressure and constraint. I wonder if this might be a useful experience to help turn Memorial Day into more than just a ritual that loses its true meaning as time goes by. The culture of free speech is shaping whole generations of immigrants and forces many to rethink and sometimes dismiss old customs. But it also allows them to ask questions about the collective memory as it developed over the years in the Netherlands, a memory that is resistant to many questions. Some of these were officially acknowledged for the first time when Queen Beatrix made an official speech for the occasion of the fiftieth anniversary of the end of the war: "For an objective account of what happened we must not conceal the fact that the occupier encountered the heroic resistance of some, as well as the passive acceptance and active support of others."

Indeed, it is true that the Netherlands is still struggling with its colonial past. What is more, if you look at it from an immigrant's point of view, it was the Europeans who colonized parts of Africa and refused to let go of these colonies even after World War II. And did the Dutch not go on the rampage in Indonesia almost immediately after they themselves had been liberated from the Germans? I still struggle to understand this behavior.

The arrival of immigrants has revived an intense discussion about freedom, safety, and especially freedom of speech. A number of minor as well as major conflicts are going on between Europeans and immigrants from countries where the events of World War II are seen in a different light. And virtually all of these conflicts trigger some association with World War II for native Europeans: statements and political programs of extreme right-wing parties remind us of Hitler's raids: never again must we repeat Auschwitz. Yet third-generation Arabs, who identify with so-called Arabs in Palestine and march in demonstrations at Amsterdam's Dam Square, chant enthusiastically: "Hamas, hamas, Jews to the gas!"

Every immigrant struggles with a divided sense of loyalty between his native country, his family and past, on the one hand, and his country of the present and future on the other. As a child I used to hear nothing but negative comments about Jews. My earliest memory dates from the time we lived in Saudi Arabia in the mid-seventies. Sometimes we would have no running water. I remember hearing my mother wholeheartedly agreeing with our neighbor that the Jews had been pernicious again. Those Jews hate Muslims so much that they'll do anything to dehydrate us. "Jew" is the worst term of abuse in both Somali and Arabic. Later, when I was a teenager and living in Somalia and Kenya, from the mid-eighties onward, every prayer we said contained a request for the extermination of the Jews. Just imagine that: five times a day. We were passionately praying for their destruction but had never actually met one. With that background experience, and my loyalty to the political, cultural, and religious variant of Islam, which I (and millions with me) inherited from my childhood, I arrived in the Netherlands. Here I came into contact with an entirely different view of the Jews: they are human beings before anything else. But what upset me more was learning about the immense injustice that had been done to the people labeled "Jews." The Holocaust and the anti-Semitism that led to it cannot be compared to any other form of ethnic cleansing. This makes the history of the Jews in Europe unique.

More understandable is the motivation and determination with which people commit genocide. The Hutus against the Tutsis in Rwanda, and the Serbians against Muslims in the former Yugoslavia are proof of how hatred can organize people and bring them to act hatefully. Such eruptions of aggression are often preceded by oppression and a lack of freedom, sometimes enforced by the government and sometimes—more and more, in fact—because there is no government to take charge. Much time and deliberation is invested beforehand in the process of cultivating and organizing the hatred that gives rise to hostile actions. Dissidents who are aware of the destructive nature of plans try to resist them; they warn others and attempt to dissuade them from joining in. For this, you need a climate with institutions that will guarantee freedom of speech.

I am not the only immigrant who has come to the Netherlands, Europe, or the West in search of freedom. There are millions like me. They come on planes through the mediation of people traffickers, having sold all their possessions to pay for the journey. Immigrants from countries with no freedom escape on trucks, walk for days on end, or float across the sea in fragile little boats. Thousands of people have died on their way to Europe.

What Europe has managed to do in the last fifty-eight years, through remembering the dead and celebrating its freedom, is to realize that freedom and the peace that comes with it demand constant effort to maintain. The enjoyment of personal identity and the acceptance of pluralism are only really possible when the rights of individuals are guaranteed. The realization that civil society means living with conflict; that to do this you need words. And that therefore the word—freedom of speech—is the key to a stable society.

It is here in Europe that immigrants like me can explore the reality of free speech without risking serious repercussions, such as banishment, imprisonment, book burning, censorship, or decapitation. Every day I discover the effect that words can have—this is painful at times. They can be hurtful and offensive, and may cause misunderstandings. But they can also clarify, explain, and generally relieve suffering. For immigrants from countries where there is no freedom of speech it will be difficult to know how to handle this freedom. Difficult but necessary.

We need words to understand the present times. We need words to come to terms with our past. Words to express that clash of loyalties we experience when we move to a new country; that feeling of being torn between two worlds. Words to describe our insights into our culture and religion, which are part of the reason we left our hearth and home.

As an immigrant who has settled in Europe, I am in a position to compare the way of life in my native country with that of my future country. In order to share my observations with other immigrants who find it difficult to adjust, I need words. I need words so that I can say that maybe the standards and values our parents brought us up with, and their religion, are not as wonderful as we always imagined.

As I said at the beginning, lately I have found myself in unfamiliar situations that have turned my life upside down. But I will never forget where that life began: at the Digfeer Hospital, in Mogadishu, now severely damaged by warfare. And I will never cease to ask myself, How many children who were born there at the same time I was have had a good life?

TEN

Four Women's Lives

In 1992, I escaped to the Netherlands, fleeing the marriage my father arranged for me to a fellow clan member in Canada. Despite my fierce protestations, my father refused to change his mind. On my way to Canada, in Germany, I seized the opportunity to run away from my family and escaped to Holland, where I was taken to the Center for Asylum Seekers. I was the only one there who could tell my fellow seekers' story in English. Two Somali girls, who were living in the same bungalow as I was, asked if I would come with them to the refugee worker and help explain their situation. Soon I was asked to go everywhere with them. They had lice, so we had to go to the medical services. I went with them to the registration office for foreigners; to the office for legal help; to various institutions responsible for social welfare. Other asylum seekers from Somalia found out about me. After a while, refugee workers advised me to take up interpreting professionally. I was doing it as a favor, and professional interpreters are paid a decent fee. At first my Dutch was not good enough. I translated from Somali into English, but they said they were not allowed to pay me for that. The refugee workers helped me out: "Just start in Dutch and if you get stuck, we'll carry on in English."

In 1993 I left the shelter for asylum seekers and applied to the Netherlands Center for Interpreters. Although I scored well in the tests, they said I would have to wait until I had been resident in the

Netherlands for at least three years. When I realized that more and more Somali people were moving to the Netherlands, I knocked on the door of the immigration and naturalization services. They added me to their list of on-call interpreters, and from then on I got plenty of work. I worked as an interpreter from 1995 to 2001. I saw dozens of men and women who had contracted sexually transmitted diseases (AIDS, syphilis, gonorrhea, chlamydia, et cetera), and many women who had gotten pregnant by accident. There is a much higher incidence of unwanted pregnancies among newcomers from third-world countries, where anything remotely sexual is still heavily taboo, than among native Westerners, who have a more liberal attitude to sex.

Here are four experiences from the time I worked as an interpreter.

"I AM NOT PREGNANT; I AM A VIRGIN"

A nineteen-year-old Somali girl goes to the Medical Services at the Refugee Center in 's-Gravendeel and complains of not feeling well. One of the doctors examines her urine and concludes she is pregnant. The doctor wants to tell her this and asks me to be an interpreter over the telephone.

Shocked, the girl breaks down in tears. I can hear her crying over the phone but cannot make out what she says. She seems utterly desperate. It gives me the shivers even to remember it.

Then she says, "But that is impossible, I am a virgin, I can't be pregnant." She continues to deny it. She says she can prove that she is a virgin: "I was stitched." She can't have done it with a boy, because the stitches are all intact.

The doctor tries to calm her down and promises he will test her urine a second time.

Not long after this I receive another phone call from the same girl and listen to the same story. The doctor tells the Somali girl that he has tested her urine again and that she really is pregnant.

He asks whether she has had any sexual education. She answers: "Why should I? I didn't need any: I was going to remain a virgin until marriage."

She tells the doctor she has been in the Netherlands only a month. A Somali boy, who has been in the Netherlands much longer and speaks Dutch, has helped her with everything. Each time she had to see her solicitor he came with her. One day he invited her and two other Somali girls to his home in Dordrecht. There he made a pass at her. He took her up to his bedroom while the two other girls remained in the sitting room. He wanted to go to bed with her and took off her clothes. He promised he would not make her lose her virginity. He kept saying that he had helped her, and that now it was her turn to do something for him.

The doctor has to drag the story out of her. She tells him that the boy did not insert his penis inside her, but merely rubbed it against her. He did ejaculate while he was on top of her, but the stitches had remained intact. They had both been convinced she was still a virgin.

The doctor explains that in order to become pregnant you need a man and a woman; that some women are more fertile than others; and that there are certain times when you are more fertile than others, depending on where you are in your menstrual cycle. She seems to have had the misfortune of being particularly fertile at that moment, which has allowed her to become pregnant, possibly through a single drop of semen.

Her reaction shows that she hasn't a clue about sexual intercourse or reproduction.

The doctor explains that she can choose from a number of options: she can keep the baby, she can have an abortion, or she can give it up for adoption.

The girl is in a complete muddle. "I've only been here a month," she cries hysterically. "I can't do this. My family set aside so much money to allow me to travel to the Netherlands, and this is how I thank them. I have disgraced them beyond belief. I can't let this happen. I must hide."

When the doctor asks if she wants an abortion—after all, the fetus is still very early in its development—she says, "No, no, no, I have disgraced myself with my family, I'm not going to disgrace myself with Allah as well, by murdering my baby." She categorically refuses to have an abortion. It is beyond discussion. "I would end up in hell."

According to Islam, an extramarital pregnancy brings great shame on the family, but you can still redeem yourself in the eyes of Allah. Abortion, though, the killing of an innocent baby, is a deadly sin, for which there is no forgiveness.

The doctor suggests that, alternatively, she can give up her baby for adoption. She briefly considers this option but dismisses it, "I made a mistake," she says, "I must carry the responsibility for it."

The doctor tells her that in that case she will have to come for regular checkups, and that she can get support from a psychotherapist if she wants. When he proposes to involve the father, she agrees, which shows that she did like the boy, after all.

THIS GIRL WAS completely clueless. She had never had any sexual education because in her culture that was deemed unnecessary. Sex before marriage is forbidden; when a woman marries she must be a virgin. Sexual education would only give people the wrong idea.

This taboo also leads to ignorance among Muslims about AIDS and how you can get it. They think it is a disease that only homosexuals, Christians, and nonbelievers can contract, not Muslims or Somalis. I interpreted for men who led active sex lives and who visited prostitutes. When they turned out to be HIV-positive, they said, "I can't be, I am a Muslim." As if the HIV virus would know the difference.

Somali girls are brought up with the motto, "Just keep your stitches intact." The moment of truth comes during the wedding night. If it turns out that your vaginal walls are no longer stitched together, you are a whore. The sewing together of the vaginal walls is not, strictly speaking, an Islamic custom. The Prophet Muhammad says in the Koran that boys should be circumcised, but no mention is made of female circumcision. The tradition of stitching is pre-Islamic but was adopted by Islam; you could compare it to what happened with the pre-Christian tradition of the Christmas tree in Christianity. Muslim scholars have never condemned the ritual of female circumcision because in Islam the importance of virginity at marriage counts so heavily. When they came into contact with this tribal ritual they must have thought, Hey, wouldn't that be a good way to guarantee a girl's virginity? Excellent! Stitching is especially popular in African Islamic countries, such as Somalia, Eritrea, Sudan, and Egypt, and also in Indonesia.

ANAB'S STORY

Anab and Shukri are two underage asylum seekers. Upon arrival in the Netherlands, they are asked whether they have any family in the country. They are sent to Sa-ied, an older half brother who has been living in the Netherlands with his wife for five years. The organization in charge of underage asylum seekers, a trust called De Opbouw, places the girls "under his care" instead of appointing an official guardian. At that time the trust was responsible for finding suitable guardians for underage asylum seekers who had come without their parents and for monitoring their general welfare.

Sa-ied subjects both girls to severe sexual abuse for an extended period of time; Anab, the eldest of the two, suffers the worst and longest. The story comes to the surface when the younger sister, Shukri, goes to the social worker at the trust and tells her everything. The trust reports the case and also contacts the child protection agency. Sa-ied is arrested and ends up in prison.

At the police headquarters of the vice squad in The Hague, I meet Anab's and Shukri's sister. I have been asked to be an interpreter for this heavily pregnant Somali woman, who is wearing a headscarf. She greets me and immediately asks, "Who do you belong to?" Which means: "From which clan are you?" I say that in my capacity of interpreter I am not allowed to answer such questions. But as I am a Somali woman, she wants to know because of the things that are going to be discussed. I refuse again, explaining that I am sworn to secrecy.

She tells the police that she, her two sisters, and her half brother are all related on their father's side. In those circumstances a half brother is seen as a full brother. The police ask her in detail about the perpetrator. Did she know that he was sexually abusing her sisters? Does he have a history of abusing women and girls? Does he always follow the same pattern? And so on. She takes half an hour or more to tell the police how perfectly virtuous her family is: that it is just this boy; that sexual abuse never occurs among Somali people; that this is a curse. Finally she demands a full investigation of the case to check whether it really happened. The woman is thoroughly confused. She wonders how she can put it right.

I find out many details about the case: when it began, how it began, who reported it, and that the man did not only abuse the two girls but regularly raped and violated his wife as well.

Approximately one week later my niece Maryan comes to live with me. At the weekend she asks me if I can pick her up from an address in Utrecht. She wants to visit a friend whom she knows from her first days in the Netherlands. They were both assigned to the care of De Opbouw, the trust in charge of underage asylum seekers, and have become friends: young girls who have fun together and enjoy wearing high heels.

At the address in Utrecht I find an unbelievable mess. The whole house stinks of urine. Two toddlers—no older than one and two years—are puttering about in nappies that they have been wearing for far too long. Dirty nappies are lying around everywhere. My niece's friend, whose house we are visiting, is called Anab. She offers us tea and disappears into the kitchen. We are kept waiting for a long time.

While I am sitting there on the sofa with Maryan, and Anab is making us tea (I suspect she cannot find anything; we never get any tea), Maryan says, "You see those videotapes over there? That's all pornography. Hard porn. Anab's husband rents them. He forces Anab to watch them and to do all the crazy things shown in the video. He rapes her anally; she has to put up with horrible things."

I recognize the story: this is the same Anab as the one I came across in the file at the police station in The Hague. While the man who raped and traumatized Anab is behind bars, her family has managed to find a cousin prepared to marry her, despite the fact that she is no longer a virgin. The sexual abuse—which, according to the sister—has "never before happened in our family"—has been swept under the carpet, and the family name has been cleared.

On inquiry it emerges that Anab was married to her cousin as soon as she reached eighteen. From that age the young asylum seekers no longer fall under the care of the Opbouw Trust. Presumably her cousin, for whatever reason, had been unable to find a wife. The family said to him: "We have a wife for you, but you'll have to keep your mouth shut about what happened to her." After years of abuse by her half brother, Anab is now suffering the abuse of her cousin, whom she has been forced to marry.

Anab ran away from home more than once, and on several occasions she was removed from the house by social services, but she went back each time. Through a neighbor she was helped to settle in a shelter for abused women for a while, until her husband picked her up and took her home. Sa-ied is in prison because he sexually abused Anab, but her husband, who treats her just as badly, remains at large.

THE FAMILY OF these two girls paid people traffickers a hefty sum of money to let their children go to school in the Netherlands. This was done in a spirit of hopeful optimism; then—inadvertently—the whole thing ended like this.

Anab's story shows how a girl is sacrificed in the name of the sacred cult of virginhood to save the family honor. And it is not just Anab who becomes the victim of this myth; her children and husband are equally affected. Her husband behaves insanely with her and tells himself it is all right, since "she had lost her virginity, so she was already a whore." And her two children literally grow up in a rubbish dump. What will become of them?

Anab's younger sister Shukri leaves for good. She escapes and never wishes to have anything to do with her family again.

THE VIRTUOUS HOUSEWIFE

She is in her mid-forties, has two children, and is pregnant with her third. The doctor tells her that he wants to discuss the result of a blood test that was done as part of a routine pregnancy examination. There is something important he needs to tell her: she is HIV-positive.

The woman is upset: "That's not true. I have led such a virtuous, chaste life. I have strictly adhered to the rules of Islam and of my family. And when I was young I never so much as looked at a boy. I have never been alone with a boy. I can't possibly have a sexually transmitted disease."

The doctor repeats that she is HIV-positive all the same and asks: "What about your husbands's sexual activities?"

She replies that her husband is very good to her, that he takes good care of the children, behaves in a responsible manner, and comes from a good family. It is out of the question that her husband could have contracted HIV. And anyway, it is a disease Muslims cannot get. It is a disease that affects Christians, and above all homosexuals. Neither she nor her husband has had a blood transfusion, so that cannot be the cause either.

When her husband is examined, it turns out that he is also HIV-positive. He moved to the Netherlands before her. She joined him later when the family was reunited. It seems likely that when he was on his own, he led an active sex life or regularly slept with prostitutes.

"AFTER THE ABORTION, I WILL NEED TO BE A VIRGIN"

I am called by a doctor. "I have little Amma here, a Somali girl," he says, "who wants to discuss something serious but refuses to see an interpreter. We've finally got her to accept an interpreter over the phone. Can you help?"

The girl refuses an interpreter because she is too ashamed to reveal her problems in the presence of another Somali woman. To win her trust I tell her that as an interpreter I am sworn to secrecy. She refuses to give her name. She is seventeen but smart for her age. When I promise her I will not pass on anything to anyone else, she says, "No, you had better not."

She says to the doctor, "I am pregnant and I want it removed."

"How do you know you're pregnant?" the doctor asks.

"I bought a predictor kit, and the test showed that I'm pregnant," she says. "I wasn't surprised because I had missed my period."

The doctor says that she is still officially underage and that he cannot just refer her to an abortion clinic. Her guardian at the trust in charge of underage asylum seekers will have to be involved in the decision.

"No," she answers. "I don't want her to know."

The doctor says that in that case he cannot help her.

"Okay," she says, "then I'll go to Rotterdam. There is a Cape Verdean woman there who can do it."

Afraid of what might happen to her in Rotterdam, the doctor gives in: "All right, I'll help you. But I insist on having an interpreter present. Because it is my duty as a doctor to explain everything to you."

She describes how her pregnancy would be regarded in the Somali community: "If they find out, I'll become an outcast." At the shelter for refugees, she shares a room with two other Somali women. To prevent them from realizing that she is pregnant, she wants the abortion to go ahead as soon as possible.

SHE ACCEPTS ME as an interpreter, and together with the doctor I visit her to explain that in the Netherlands you need to follow certain procedures before you can have an abortion. We ask her to allow herself two days to think carefully about all the questions she will have to answer ("How long have you been pregnant?" "Do you wish the father to be involved?"). She needs to let everything sink in before making a final decision. She must be absolutely certain that she wants to have the abortion. But she has already made up her mind it seems. She is referred to the abortion clinic in Leiden, and I accompany her.

The waiting room in the clinic is full of immigrant women. The so-called recovery rooms are also almost exclusively filled with immigrants, mainly from Turkey and Morocco and a few from China. The girl for whom I am interpreting is asked the same questions as before and she is encouraged to think carefully about her decision. Asked whether she would like the father to be present, she replies, "No, he gave me his word that he wouldn't penetrate me, but he did. I don't want him involved."

She demands that her stitches not be damaged by the abortion. They must absolutely remain intact. The doctor examines the stitches and says he will have to take them out. "In that case I want you to put new stitches in after the abortion," she demands, and proceeds to have the abortion.

After the abortion the girl is told that she will have to recover first and can come back at a later date for the stitches. Presumably this never happened, since Dutch doctors will not replace these kinds of stitches. But to have the stitches replaced; she might have traveled to Italy or the United Kingdom, where doctors are known to do this.

·   ·   ·

THE DUTCH SOCIAL security system is not very well set up for the problems of Muslims. This inadvertently contributes to perpetuating the situation and keeps everyone locked in the virgins' cage. Dutch psychologists are, quite rightly, used to treating their patients as individuals. In my interpreting days I witnessed how they also used this approach with Muslim women. An important question was always: "What would you like yourself?" Many women simply did not know. They would sit, quiet as a mouse, and shrug their shoulders. "What my husband wants," they might say timidly, or "As Allah wishes." And there were even women who would answer: "Whatever you think is right." They had never learned to want anything for themselves. "What would you like for your children? What decision would you like to take for them?" They had not learned this either, so did not know how to answer. The social workers did not understand them; they were puzzled and frustrated. As a last resort they referred these women to other agencies, but there is a limit to how often this can be done.

There is a new branch within the world of aid agencies known as "intercultural welfare" (or something similarly ugly). It offers separate help to, for example, Muslim women who have suffered abuse. One example is the Saadet Shelter in Rotterdam. The women who end up there do not learn how to become more resilient and independent. No, assertiveness training is only given to native Dutch victims of abuse. The preferred solution for immigrant women is "mediation" between the victim, her family, and her husband. This common attitude of the aid agencies is based on the advice of countless organizations set up for the benefit of the immigrant population, some ethnic in origin, others religious. The spokespeople for these organizations, which are subsidized by the government, tend to be men and occasionally women who for one reason or another wish to maintain the status quo.

ELEVEN

How to Deal with Domestic Violence More Effectively

An average of eighty women, forty children, and twenty-five men die each year in the Netherlands as a result of domestic violence, but the government has no proper answer to the problem. If the domestic violence takes place among people from a "different culture," the authorities are extra reluctant to intervene, and clear choices cannot be made.

Plenty of mission statements have been produced in recent years. Apart from perfunctory declarations disapproving of and condemning violence, numerous promises have been made over the years to the Dutch House of Representatives, reports are published at regular intervals, and domestic violence has been the theme of dozens of symposia and conferences. The above figures come from a report circulated in March 2002 by the then outgoing government. At an international level the Dutch government even managed to get a resolution on honor killings accepted by the General Assembly of the United Nations. This resolution calls on member states to "take preventive action against this kind of crime and to combat it, through legislative, educational, social, and other measures." This is all rather unconvincing when you realize that none of the successive cabinets have managed to turn their declarations of intent into actual policy. Since the initial acceptance of the motion against domestic violence, in 1981, no coherent plan of action has been proposed, and the campaign against domestic terror is still unformed, insubstantial, and ineffectual.

Despite several studies, the Counsel for the Prosecution has no idea, for example, how often honor killings occur in the Netherlands, because the police still record them as homicides. We also know far too little about genital mutilation of women and forced marriage. An added problem when dealing with domestic violence is that different cultures do not necessarily view it in the same light. Because the native Dutch population generally regards domestic violence as immoral, the approach of certain local authorities, to subject perpetrators of domestic violence to a fixed plan of treatment, has had some good results. Sadly, however, the government has not been able to develop these local methods (a good example is Utrecht) into one national policy.

THE MURDER OF Zarife, a Turkish girl, living in the Dutch city of Almelo, by her father, illustrates a category of domestic violence that is tolerated on cultural or religious grounds. The offender's conduct is morally acceptable within his own community. What is more, the offender will often feel under pressure from others to use violence. If he fails to fulfill his duty, he can be literally "gossiped out" of the community. An offender who takes action with the knowledge and approval of his family and saves his honor, actually goes up in the estimation of his community. For the girls and women in this culture this is a strong deterrent, which thwarts the government's emancipation policies.

At the root of the problem is the Islamic concept of premarital sex. What we need is a coherent cultural campaign to promote discussion about sexuality. Sex before marriage, as long as it is between adults, is not illegal. And although you may disagree about whether this is morally acceptable or not, violence should not be the response under any circumstances.

It is naive to think that organizations representing the target groups should lead such a campaign. Dutch social workers who take advice from these organizations are inclined to disguise the real issue. They reassure the parents of girls who have been threatened that their daughters are chaste virgins, while at the same time their colleagues in the medical clinics are helping girls to have their hymens restored.

Everybody agrees that domestic violence is a highly complex issue, but the Dutch government's approach to the problem is just too fragmented. At least six departments dealing with no fewer than twenty-one laws are involved. At the local government level is a jungle of institutions, each responsible for a different aspect of domestic violence. Thus, there are different organizations for each of the following: identifying and reporting domestic violence, investigating the crime, supporting the victim, tracking down offenders, prosecuting, and preventing. None of these organizations sees it as its main task to prevent and tackle domestic violence. In this labyrinth a victim will feel easily lost. She already needs all her courage and strength to break away from the violent environment, for fear of further violence shrouds the problem in shame and secrecy.

In April 2003 the House of Representatives accepted a motion that demanded that the government set out its vision for the campaign against domestic violence by September 1 of that year. Typical of what normally happens, the presentation of this plan has so far been postponed twice.

In order to tackle domestic violence, a number of measures need to be in place.

- There should be a central help desk for victims, one service that coordinates all the organizations involved. This institution should be responsible for the preventing, identifying, and reporting domestic violence, referring those involved, gathering information, giving advice, tracking down offenders, preparation for the prosecution, and probation. Utrecht is one of the places that has had good experiences with a coordinated service along these lines, although the various links in the chain of preventive measures remain spread over a number of institutions.

- The overall budget and coordination should be in the hands of one government minister or secretary.

- The safety of the victims must be guaranteed by placing the offender, rather than the victims, outside the home, and by legally obliging the offender to undergo treatment.

The emphasis should move from aftercare to prevention. Following the example of the United States, the Netherlands should set up family courts that specialize in the criminal prosecution of perpetrators of domestic violence. The benefits of this approach lie in the fact that collaboration between police, the public prosecution, and social services can be speeded up, and thus become more pragmatic, efficient, and cost-effective. Moreover, this would, at last, allow us to measure the result of the government's policy. Finally, a more effective approach to dealing with domestic violence will be a positive influence on the problems of the oppression of women and underage delinquency. How many women will have to undergo Zarife's fate before the government can fight domestic violence effectively?

POSTSCRIPT: THE STATE OF AFFAIRS IN JULY 2004

Since this chapter was first written, a majority of the elected members of the House of Representatives has voted in favor of registering honor killings and domestic violence on the basis of ethnic origin. This should finally allow more insight into the problem. Recently, a report commissioned by the Ministry of Justice revealed that one in four women will experience domestic violence at some point. I suspect that the true figure is higher, as corporal punishment is seen as justifiable on educational grounds by most families from Muslim countries.

Minister of Justice Piet Hein Donner has said, under pressure from the House of Representatives, that he will consider appointing a committee that will look at how accessories to the crime (from the wider family) who may have assisted in (the planning of) an honor killing could be brought to trial.

Minister of Social Affairs Aart-Jan de Geus and Minister of Integration and Immigration Rita Verdonk have agreed that by the end of this government's term, there will be a structure that covers the nation (i.e., a national help desk), allowing the government to clamp down on domestic violence more effectively. The ministers have promised to see to it that culturally legitimized violence against women in immigrant circles will be firmly dealt with.

In addition, the present government has promised to take prompter and more effective measures against the trafficking of people. This kind of trade is a monstrous and well-hidden form of violence against women. Girls (from as young as eight years old in Asian countries) and women are kidnapped or lured away from their birthplaces in poor regions (Albania, the former Yugoslavia, Azerbaijan, Afghanistan, Tajikistan, Chechnya, Sierra Leone, Sudan, Congo, various countries in Latin America, China, Vietnam, the Philippines, et cetera) to be sold as sex slaves and exploited in the rich West. Asylum seekers who have been refused a residence permit are enticed by pimps, who promise them "work" and then send them to the red-light districts of European cities, where they are forced to offer themselves as prostitutes. The money earned by these women goes to the so-called organized crime networks. An unintended effect of European asylum policy in combination with the constant stream of immigrants arriving from non-Western countries, is that countless girls fall victim to the sex industry. Given the international character of the trafficking in women, a joint plan of action from the European countries is called for. The harmonization of European asylum policies would at least allow us to get a clearer picture of the scale of the trade in women. It is precisely in this area that a joint European approach is so necessary.

TWELVE

Genital Mutilation Must Not Be Tolerated

Genital mutilation of girls is sometimes referred to as "circumcision." Implicitly, this likens it to male circumcision. If male circumcision meant removing the glans and testicles, and adhering the remains of the penis to the empty sac, the comparison would be valid. It is not valid. "Circumcision" is a term that implies that the practice is acceptable. It is not acceptable. Nor is it culturally "excusable."

Genital mutilation of girls is the most underestimated violation of human rights and women's rights worldwide. In 2002, according to Amnesty International reports, between 1 million and 1.4 million girls were robbed of their genitals. The international community is more gripped by the spread of the HIV virus and AIDS than by the atrocious practice of genital mutilation in girls. Yet the health complications that circumcised women suffer are shocking, pernicious, and widespread. For instance, working in Ghana, Dutch urologist Hans de Wall was visited by an utterly distraught twenty-six-year-old woman who had been circumcised with a piece of broken glass when she was ten. Since the birth of a stillborn child, the woman had been constantly leaking urine and feces because of fistulas. These fistulas often develop when women have trouble giving birth due to the mutilation of their bodies, the narrowing of the vaginal canal. The mutilation also endangers the infants in their passage through the birth canal. Many first-time mothers are unable to labor successfully and the babies get stuck in their mother's artificially narrowed birth canal. Some babies die as a result; some have birth-related handicaps and injuries.

The pressure of the stuck baby on the mother's internal tissues cuts off the blood supply, damaging the tissues and nerves—including nerves of the legs, leading to lameness—and also can rip holes in their urethras and bowels. The women suffer the grief of losing their babies—because of a cruel mutilation of their own bodies over which they had no control—and also suffer from the trauma of their internal injuries, which leave them completely incontinent.

Women with obstetric fistulas number in the millions, according to the World Health Organization. And there are few doctors who can care for them. Often cast off by their families, abandoned, impoverished, embarrassed by their condition, they wait years for an operation to correct the fistula—*if* they can get to a medical center that does the procedure. Many suffer in silence and shame. Their isolation and disownment are not even a blip on their governments' radar screens.

According to a story in the *New York Times,* more than a third of one doctor's patients in Nigeria are fifteen or younger; almost another third are between fifteen and twenty; most were married before they had menstruated, at eleven or twelve. Even doctors who devote themselves to corrective surgery for obstetric fistulas cannot keep up with the demand for their services. And even after fistulas are repaired, labor with another baby can create new ones. Genital mutilation of girls leads to inevitable, later mutilations when the women are grown.

As with other forms of appalling violence against women, genital mutilation tends to stay in the sphere of public condemnation, United Nations resolutions, and other paper weapons. Concrete measures that would lead to banishing these practices seem a long way off. People have clung to the belief that, over time, the problem would disappear by itself, with economic development and the increasing availability of information and advice. Other concerns such as poverty, war, natural disasters, and AIDS are given a higher priority in these countries because of their more visible, immediate impact on the population as a whole.

In rich countries, where such calamities do not absorb all the attention, genital mutilation is associated with immigrants. When first brought to the public's attention, it evoked shocked reactions. In the Netherlands, for example, the practice was immediately condemned and made a criminal offense. However, this has not stopped parents from Africa and parts of Asia from mutilating their daughters in the Netherlands or elsewhere in Europe. Moreover, the government is well aware that these parents take their daughters back to their country of origin in order to subject them to the ritual of mutilation there. There is no excuse for tolerating this practice.

A medical report for the government advised the government to combat female circumcision first of all through preventive measures and by an information campaign, using legal sanctions only as a secondary aid. However, enforcement of the law is of primary importance because of the gravity of the offense and the serious implications for the victims. So my party and I are in favor of introducing a screening program that could help prevent female circumcision. Girls from "high-risk countries" should be checked once a year to see if they have been circumcised.

In the present debate in the Netherlands about how genital mutilation should be stopped, some argue that it should be assigned a separate heading in the criminal code. This change could be interpreted to mean that genital mutilation is not formally against the law now, which sends the wrong message to those who inflict it on girls. Others call for a more "open discussion" of mutilation within the immigrant community, and a third group believes that if people are educated about the consequences of mutilation, they will stop.

In my view, the fight against genital mutilation, in the Netherlands and other countries such as Canada and the United States, is primarily a matter of enforcing the law. After all, genital mutilation falls under the criminal offense of "willful, grievous bodily harm" as well as an "unqualified practice of medicine." Under our law, a doctor who has circumcised a woman, or assisted in such a procedure, can be brought before the medical disciplinary tribunal. Moreover, genital mutilation of girls falls under the definition of child abuse.

It is notable that no arrests have been made to date in spite of there being good reason to believe that girls who are normally resident in the Netherlands are subjected to ritual mutilation during the summer holidays, either in the Netherlands or abroad. It seems unacceptable, under the circumstances, that there is no monitoring of this serious crime. The Dutch government's attitude toward genital mutilation seems to be one of passive tolerance: genital mutilation is prohibited by law, but in practice, the authorities turn a blind eye. Following up all the recommendations of the government medical report, management and coordination of all the institutions involved in the fight against genital mutilation, and facilitating dialogue and debate in the ethnic communities that practice genital mutilation do not necessarily guarantee that the parents of the girls at risk will comply with the law.

The government should be committed to introducing a screening program because it regards safety and the enforcement of law as two of its highest priorities. In the 2004 budget for the Department of Justice, we read: "An important contributory factor to public safety is that citizens observe the laws, as the majority will tend to do." And a little further on: "it has been noted that enforcement of the law is unsatisfactory. This should be improved in the coming years." In its proposal for a safety program to help girls at risk of mutilation the cabinet moreover declares its intention to focus on prosecuting graver crimes and "giving priority to the victims of crimes with a serious impact."

Genital mutilation falls into the category of extremely serious crimes and has a substantial negative health impact—even a crippling effect—on the victim. Its consequences include: "shock, bleeding, abscess formation; and at a later stage, complications affecting the urinary tract, as well as labor and delivery; psychiatric, psychosomatic, and psychosocial effects for young girls . . . After the procedure girls can become introverted, reticent, withdrawn, and may show signs of behavioral disturbances such as eating disorders and phobias." Genital mutilation can also "lead to posttraumatic stress disorder. For the girl experiences a sense of powerlessness, a lack of control, consent, and information, and suffers intense pain."

Are there openings in the law for the introduction of a screening program?

Article 11 of the Dutch constitution guarantees the inviolability of the individual's human body. This article is the little brother of Article 10 of the constitution, which safeguards the individual's right to personal privacy. Both articles matter for our proposal; in terms of international treaty law, they are the counterparts of Article 8 of the European Convention on Human Rights (ECHM) and Article 17 of the United Nations Covenant on Civil and Political Rights (signed in 1966).

Yet Muslim reactionaries as well as all other political parties and politically correct politicians who want to preserve genital mutilation argue *against* a screening program. Their sophistic contention is that a compulsory checkup for a young at-risk girl is a medical intervention that encroaches on the right to the inviolability of the individual's (the girl's) body and encroaches on the girl's and the parents' right to personal privacy.

The ECHM outlines in detail how and under what circumstances the government may lawfully breach the constitution. It is essential that there are enough compelling reasons for such a transgression, otherwise it becomes pointless to have a constitution. The ECHM lists a number of grounds on which the government has the right to breach the constitution. They are (freely translated): border security, public security, national economic welfare, the prevention of national disarray and penal offenses, the protection of health and moral standards, and the protection of individual rights.

In other words, a breach of the constitution can be justified if it prevents the occurrence of a crime (willful, grievous bodily harm). This exceptional ground seems the obvious argument on which to build our case. The ECHM offers the possibility of lawfully impos- ing medical treatment, provided it can be demonstrated that doing so is of vital importance in the prevention of crime.

Proportionality is one aspect of this "demonstrating it is of vital importance." Is the violation of individual rights outweighed by the importance of preventing the crime? In other words: does the end justify the means?

The legal debate about how best to combat genital mutilation centers on this question. I believe that without compulsory screen- ing there is no effective way of preventing genital mutilation. There- fore, the program is a necessary step. Moreover, the constitution requires the government to take preventive measures in order to protect the integrity of the human body. It gives the government the duty to act.

My party and I are instructing the government to take steps that will prevent genital mutilation. Regarding the question of propor- tionality, an annual examination by a female nurse working for the local health authority is vastly preferable to allowing girls to be put at risk of serious mutilation. This legal argument far outweighs the main objections against medical examination.

Yet another sophistic legal objection against the introduction of a screening program is that it contradicts our constitution by singling out a specific group to be screened and not the entire Dutch popu- lation. These obstructionists argue that imposing a compulsory medical examination on a group of people from high-risk countries is a form of discrimination.

Other antagonists argue that the intrusion of an annual screen- ing test stigmatizes the parents and so also becomes a heavy burden for the child. These people do not think that the introduction of compulsory screening is proportional to the crime. Other antago- nists illogically argue that there is no reason to suppose that somebody from a country with a high incidence of genital mutilation is automatically going to become involved in mutilation in the Netherlands—despite ample evidence to the contrary.

I say that the consequences of genital mutilation are so inimical to the well-being of the child that the government should give priority to its duty to act to protect someone from harm. We also believe that even if the risk of genital mutilation is not great, preventive measures are still needed in the light of what might happen and has happened. Female children whose parents come from high-risk countries do in fact run a very real risk of being mutilated because many parents still attach tremendous importance to the tradition.

The government medical report recorded evidence that young girls are subjected to mutilation during school vacations. Because of the hidden effects of the ritual—genitals are by definition covered parts of the body—society can disapprove of the ritual while at the same time denying that it is a problem. If children had their noses, or part of their ears cut off, the government would not be able to get away with its policy of passive tolerance.

Genital mutilation cannot be done legally; parents in the Netherlands know that it is against the law, which is why they have it done during the long school vacation and sometimes in their home country. In doing so, they know that the girl can recover from her injuries without having to explain anything to the outside world. Closed groups, who live in the superstitious conviction that mutilation is good for a child, cannot be expected to be open about such matters. As a result of their conviction, the parents perceive mutilation of their own child not as a criminal activity but as an act of love, a parental duty to their daughter and to their immediate circle.

The government needs to weigh the importance of the parents' right to privacy against the child's right to health. Given the gravity of genital mutilation, my party and I would opt for the protection of the child. The services involved in the screening, such as the local health authorities, would treat all information concerning the children and their parents discreetly and protect them.

Merely declaring that the practice of genital mutilation is despicable and degrading is not going to solve the problem. It has not done so thus far, certainly. The preventive effects of education are very limited and almost impossible to measure because of the hidden character and historical nature of the practice. The pressure on immigrants from family in the home countries (family ties are not severed by geographical borders) is too strong to be overcome merely through the provision of information and education. The argument that the tradition will eventually fall away, or that the practice will die out in the Netherlands because it is against the law, is unrealistic.

The proposal for a screening program may not be perfect, but it offers maximum results if the government enforces the law to abolish these abominable practices. It has the advantage of being clear to the parents: they know exactly what to expect. And it has two positive side effects: first, it encourages targeted, efficient delivery of information and education that otherwise would be ineffective and too diffuse. Second, it can make the Netherlands a role model for Europe and the rest of the world, and help eradicate genital mutilation on other continents as well.

PROPOSAL FOR A SCREENING PROGRAM

For a screening program to prevent female circumcision, the government should take the following steps:

- With the help of Amnesty International and the United Nations, draw up a list of high-risk countries.

- Establish a program of compulsory medical examinations for children from these countries.

- Make two lists: List A should contain the names of the girls who have already been subjected to mutilation, while List B should have the names of those who have not been harmed yet. Newborn girls are automatically added to List B.

- Girls on List A are offered medical and psychological support.

- Parents of girls on List B under eighteen are called up every year for a compulsory examination of their daughter.

- Newly arrived immigrants from high-risk countries are automatically called.

- The screening can be done by the local health service. If a girl on List B turns out to have been mutilated, this has to be reported to the Child Welfare Council, which will institute proceedings against the parents.

POSTSCRIPT

After much discussion about the pros and cons of screening tests, I secured a majority in the Dutch House of Representatives, thanks to the backing of the Labor Party, a social democrat party, which is in favor of periodic screening. Although the Labor representatives eventually gave unanimous support, this might not have happened without the support of Ella Kalsbeek, a member of parliament for the Labor Party, the party I left, who played a leading role. From the very outset of this debate the minister of health, Hans Hoogervorst, expressed his absolute horror of genital mutilation, considering it a form of child abuse, and showed himself in favor of introducing a screening program as soon as possible. In April 2004, he announced the establishment of a special committee with the Public Health Board to investigate the possibility of an effective screening program and to consider how the law can be used more effectively to identify incidents. Under Dutch law it could have become possible to prosecute not only Dutch citizens, but also foreigners with a fixed place of abode in the Netherlands who have assisted in or encouraged genital mutilation abroad in countries such as Somalia, where it is allowed, or countries where it is forbidden.

To my disappointment, the committee ultimately recommended that screening not be done. The minister of health said he would not want to make screening compulsory but will offer high-risk communities the opportunity to have their children examined. Before the family is approached with this opportunity, however, the government must establish that the family is likely to practice female genital mutilation. The government will look at whether the family is from a high-risk country, if the mother of the child is circumcised herself (which can only be known if she has given birth to the girl in Holland and her status is known by a Dutch medical doctor or health worker).

I have no majority for my screening proposal. I have only my party standing with me. The program that the government has devised instead of the one we advised is a very expensive, inefficient system. Tragically, many Muslim immigrant girls will fall through the cracks.

THIRTEEN

Ten Tips for Muslim Women Who Want to Leave

Since the early 1990s, there has been a gradual but noticeable increase in the number of Muslim girls in women's shelters and special refuge centers for abused women. The shelters have been there for decades. Some of these women have successfully completed their schooling and hope to continue their education at college but have been refused permission to leave home. Their parents have not prepared them for a life of independence, and the whole family is shocked when the daughter announces she has ambitions of her own, which they regard as an alarming aberration.

A married Muslim woman who wants to leave her husband and lead an independent existence is also considered aberrant and is warned that she is making a huge mistake, not only by her husband and his family, but by her own family. If the families do manage to persuade the woman to change her mind and stay with her husband, the marital tension can sometimes be resolved peacefully. But it is not unusual for a family to respond violently to the woman's perceived betrayal of her husband. The degree and seriousness of the violence varies from case to case.

Occasionally Muslim girls run away from home in a panic. This can have unfortunate consequences. Often these girls end up in a shelter and remain dependent on public assistance for a long time. In some cases a social worker may try to mediate between the "runaway"—a peculiar term for an adult woman who wants to set up house independently—and her family, which frequently results in the woman's return home to whatever abuse caused her to panic and flee. Her family will forever treat her as an underage girl, even when she is well over forty. To them she remains a "runaway" woman.

Some Muslim girls and women who have fled their homes go off the rails. Having been brought up under strict conditions, they celebrate their freedom by going out night after night and become addicted to drugs and nightlife. These girls are targeted by the "lover boys," who entrap them in this low life. Often their lives end tragically: they feel desperately trapped and commit suicide. Some are "caught out" at the moment they decide to leave home, or shortly after, and then the nightmare of abuse begins all over again. Some girls are even lured back to their parents' place of birth with a holiday invitation, but once they get there, they are stripped of their passports and cannot escape. In the worst scenario they may be killed, as happened to the Turkish girl Zarife from the Dutch town of Almelo.

THE MANY SAD stories of women who ran away inspired me to write the following open letter, which contains ten tips for Muslim women who want to leave.

Dear Muslim Woman,

The tips that follow are not intended for all Muslim women. They are intended just for you—you who would like to have an independent life and are being stopped by your family, your husband, or your congregation. You want to leave your family or your husband because you want to take charge of your life. You want to earn your own money in order to support and maintain yourself. You wish to choose your (life) partner yourself. You are convinced that you—and not your parents, congregation, or anyone else—must decide if, and when, you get married and to whom. Whether you want children, and how many, is your affair. At what age you have them and how you are going to bring them up is something you want to determine yourself. You want to choose your own friends and not feel restricted to the circle you happen to belong to as a result of your birth; you are open to making contacts outside this small circle. You want to travel and discover the world. You don't want to spend the rest of your life bearing the children of a husband you don't even love; cleaning, doing the shopping, and cooking three times a day; serving tea and baking cookies each weekend for people who have no interest in you; doing the washing and ironing, talking about curtain patterns, and hemming sheets. You no longer want to spend your free time with women who do nothing but gossip. You are fed up with your sisters and cousins who refuse to use their mental capacities for anything but the creation of yet another perfect recipe for cookies. You have been to enough weddings at which the girls boast not about their artistic and cultural achievements, but about the henna tattoos they applied to the palms of brides who have since disappeared into their arranged marriages. You have seen the trap into which the bride and bridegroom fall after the three days of wedding festivities.

You know you are worth more than this! You think and dream about your freedom. You would like to go outside, feel the sun on your skin and the wind in your hair. You no longer tolerate the oppression you feel in your parents' or husband's house, and you have come to the conclusion that you want to leave. The following tips, insofar as they have not occurred to you yet, may be of use.

THE PREPARATION

1. *Freedom Is a Choice*

Ask yourself these questions: Do I really want to leave? Why do I want to leave? Are there no other options? Check whether mediation is a possibility. You want the choice to leave your parents' home or your husband's to be based on more than just dissatisfaction with the present situation at home. For there will be serious repercussions if you leave, although the consequences are possibly more serious if you stay. You must, therefore, take the time to answer these questions honestly for yourself. Undoubtedly, you love your family. Yet you must be ready to accept that your actions will make your parents sad. You will be blamed for disgracing them and upsetting the whole family. Your family will do absolutely everything in their power to get you back: they will try to talk you into changing your mind, threaten to ostracize you, tell you that you have incurred a curse, and possibly use violence. Do not underestimate the power of this kind of emotional and moral blackmail. You will have to put up with comments of this kind. "Since you left, Mummy has become so ill that she can't sleep anymore." Or, "Your father is so depressed and ashamed he has trouble going to work or seeing the rest of the family." Or, "You are ruining your sister's chance to marry into a good family." Or, "Your little brother was beaten up yesterday when he tried to defend your character." Prepare yourself.

Explore your options. Take a good look at your position at home. Make a list of all the risks. You are particularly at risk if you come from a large family with a relatively high number of men who are deeply attached to their sense of honor and insist on strict religious principles. If your father happens to be an important man in the family, you are at an even bigger risk. If, on the other hand, you come from a family with a strong sense of honor but relatively few men, you are in a better position. But be careful not to underestimate the power of women's gossip to influence both sexes: they will pass on everything and turn the men against you.

If you know how the grapevine works—who will talk to whom about what, what is frowned upon, et cetera—then you can protect yourself by making sure that you do not become the subject of the gossip. This is important if you want to succeed.

Confront your own weaknesses: How good is your health? What is your temperament like: are you hot-tempered, or do you have good self-control, and do you adjust well to new situations? If you have good self-control, you are more likely to leave well prepared (and to persevere). Remember, self-control and self-sufficiency are things you can learn.

Think about how you can keep your plans hidden for as long as possible: How much time do you get to yourself each day? Does your family notice if you are gone for a few hours? Are you good at thinking up convincing excuses, at telling your parents what they want to hear? Should you perhaps wear a headscarf in order to "keep the peace" until you leave?

Realize that once you have left, you will not be able to go back (at least not for a while). And you should not go back, no matter what they say and promise. You will be in more danger from them *after* you return—possibly fatal danger. So the most important question you need to ask yourself is, Do I really want to leave?

2. Faith

You have decided that you want to live on your own. You will need to have faith. To begin with, you need to have faith in yourself. You will have moments of doubt, fear, and even regret. This is normal. After all, you are about to leave behind everything that is familiar to you (no matter how horrible your home is at times). You may never see your family again. Expect to feel besieged by doubts, but remember also that what you are doing is for your own good. The way in which you want to live cannot be combined with how your family wants you to live. Have faith in yourself.

You also need to have faith in others. Be sure to know whom you can trust. Choose someone from outside the congregation, a mature person who looks after his or her own affairs well. This should be someone who helps you to become independent, who can let you know when you are on the right road; someone who genuinely supports you and lays no claims on you; someone who won't mind if you make a mistake. The world outside is not a big, bad world. Do not mistrust everyone, but do be critical and cautious.

3. Friends

It is vital that you make friends before you abandon your family. You will not survive without friends. Establish new friendships well in advance of your departure—close friendships with people you can trust. You are starting out on a new life, and meeting new people is an important part of the experience. Of course, there will be relatives, or other fellow Muslims, who will understand your situation and pretend to be supportive, but the chances are that they will not really try to help you. These people are part of the community and tell each other everything. If one of them shows you understanding and support, it is still possible that that person will give away something in an unguarded moment. And it is not fair to burden someone with conflicting loyalties. Before you know it, your plans to leave will become common knowledge. So be vigilant. I am not saying that you cannot have any Muslim friends, but do not confide your plan to any of them. You simply cannot afford to take the risk. The consequences could be too damaging for you.

Friendship means reciprocity. Invest in your friends. Let them know that they can trust you too, that you will be there for them if they need you. Your new friends will often have different opinions about women than your family's and community's, and they may not understand you at first. Explain to them what guilt and shame mean in your family and community. Learn to be honest: you are allowed to admit mistakes; you don't have to lie about friends, dates, et cetera.

4. Address

When you leave home you will need somewhere to live. As a student or housewife, you have little disposable income. You may never have had an income in your own name. In addition, you will need to avoid any areas where people might recognize you, people who could pass on information to your parents or other relatives. Because you have little money and need to take extra safety precautions, your choice of places to live is limited. Do not hesitate to ask friends and the people you trust to help you.

University cities and towns are an attractive option because you can find cheap, safe housing there. Student accommodation tends to be accepted and common and the rent is relatively low. The only disadvantage is that you have to be registered as a student before you can move into such accommodation. In some student houses potential candidates competing for a vacant room are required to come for a "preliminary visit" in order to be approved by the rest of the occupants. Obviously, you can be unlucky and not get their approval.

If you are not a student, or have picked a university town with a shortage of student accommodations, you have other possibilities. There are couples or people who live alone, who are keen to let a room cheaply to single people with little money, preferably women. Often they are looking for someone on a short-term basis because their own children have left home or they have lost a partner. In these houses you will have to obey the landlord's rules, but you can discuss in advance the kind of privacy you will need and make your boundaries clear. Some cities, like Amsterdam, have cheap housing to rent in areas that are safe for you. These houses or apartments are reserved, on a charitable basis, for specific groups with low incomes, such as artists and musicians.

Once you have managed to find a room or apartment, make sure you move in promptly. Figure out in advance your schedule for leaving your family and finding your new home. Make sure your room is not left vacant for months on end. That would be a waste of money.

Once you have left, be careful not to give your address or telephone number to people you do not really know. Nowadays e-mail is a good way of staying in touch without giving away your address.

5. Safety

If you have been threatened by your family—before or after you've left them—you need to think carefully about the city where you want to live. If you can, choose a place where you will stand out as little as possible. If you are going to attend a college, you will be living in a city or town; if you want to find a job, then you'll want to find a smaller place, far away from your parents, that will offer you better protection and opportunities. Most cities have women's shelters and mental health services that can help you.

When you register yourself in your new place of residence, ask to speak to a special civil servant (in the United States, someone from the local department of social services) who is familiar with the predicament of a girl like you, who has known of or helped other girls who want to set up on their own and are terrified of being hunted down by their brothers, husbands, or fathers. It is vital that your address remain secret. Go to the police and report your situation. In Holland, you can use your registration form to encode your tax number, insurance, and other administrative details, as well as personal details required by the local council. Find out how to get legal help in case you need it.

Make sure that your flatmates, colleagues, and friends are informed of the potential danger you are in. You are on the run, and they must be vigilant on your behalf. It is important that no one give away your address.

6. Income

Make arrangements for how you will have income before leaving. If you want to go to college, apply for a student scholarship on time. Give a temporary address—a friend's, for example—if you have not found a place of your own yet. If you do not intend to go to college, apply for social security benefits in the place you are moving to. Doing this will oblige you to find a job, or to follow a citizenship course and explore the job market. You must not delay with any of this. While you are still at home, acquaint yourself with the (part-time) job market in your future hometown. Put your name down for (part-time) jobs and avoid taking loans and accumulating debts as much as you can.

The most important thing is to be sensible with money; there are courses that can teach you how to draw up a budget and stick to it. The local social service department will be able to point you in the right direction.

7. *Opportunities for Education*

It is good to have a part-time job, but make sure that you pass your school exams. You can come up with all kinds of excuses to miss lectures, but try not to let this happen all the time. A diploma in your pocket opens the door to long-term independence. Try to broaden your opportunities for learning new things as much as you can. Your course may require you to do a practical training. Make the best possible use of this: organize your placement in advance; negotiate how your expenses are going to be paid, how many hours you will be working per day, and how many credit points you will receive at the end of your training.

If you struggle with your workload, go to your study supervisor or mentor, who can show you study techniques, how to cram for exams and write papers. In order to get your degree, you need to have self-discipline: organize your time efficiently, go to bed on time, and plan the tasks ahead.

As a student, you will also learn how to socialize with people from outside your own religious circuit: you will need to learn what they might expect from you, as well as the unwritten rules of social etiquette. Join a student organization, go on drink dates, or to parties (you do not have to drink alcohol).

8. *Your Possessions*

You cannot take all your belongings with you when you leave: your imminent departure has to remain a secret, so you cannot take any large or bulky objects with you, such as your bed, a table, a chair, or the whole of your wardrobe. You will have to be selective and take only things you will really need. Remember to take a few precious photos and your wallet or savings, bankbook, checkbook, piggy bank, or moneybox. Do not forget your passport. You must smuggle these things out of your home piecemeal: if you are spotted leaving the house with heavy bags, or your closet is suddenly half empty, you will draw attention.

You will have to furnish your new dwelling yourself, so find out where the best secondhand shops are.

9. *State of Mind*

Leaving is a big challenge. You feel strong, you are looking forward to the moment, but at the same time you are very vulnerable. You will experience a dip in your emotional high and feel lonely; not everybody will be understanding, and that includes some of your new friends. The person in whom you have put your trust can help you strengthen your inner resilience. Remember that, even with all the help from others, you remain on your own, you are responsible for yourself. Expect there to be good and bad days, do not talk yourself down, and do not feel sorry for yourself. You will want to contact your family because you miss the warmth, the cousins, and the familiarity. Every family has its important moments: birthdays, funerals, Eid, and so on. You will feel extra lonely on these days. But bear in mind that getting in touch with your family can have serious consequences. Calls and letters can be traced.

There are consolations, though. Plenty of women like you have managed to reestablish good contact with their families. But this often takes years. You absolutely must wait until you are self-reliant financially and emotionally. You must have found a job to be able to keep yourself strong so that you can resist their complaints and urgings that you should come home. You need to be able to stop your ears against the emotional blackmail they may try on you.

10. *The Moment of Departure*

You have taken care of everything. You are still certain you are doing the right thing. You have good friends who are ready to help you. You believe in yourself, your friends, and the future. You have an address, an income, and you have enrolled yourself as a student. Perhaps you are still at school or halfway through college. You have secretly smuggled your most valued possessions out of the house. You are sure no one has noticed. Your behavior has been exemplary, and the day of your departure has finally come. The weather is fine, or perhaps it is raining. Tonight you will sleep at your new address—your room or whatever—for the very first time. But wait: how are you actually going to leave? Are you simply going to walk out and pull the door behind you without so much as a good-bye?

Yes, you are, because you must avoid drawing attention to yourself.

AND THEN YOU are gone.

What happens next?

Your parents do not know where you are and will be worried. They will need to be reassured that you left of your own accord. Before you go, write them a letter in which you explain that you love them, but that your plans for your life differ from theirs; that you respect the way they live but want to go your own way. You can mail it immediately when you leave so it can't be traced to your new location.

Call them, eventually. You will want to get in touch with them from time to time, but make sure your number cannot be traced: call from a public phone or somewhere without number recognition. It can be good to call from a public place with plenty of people around you. That way you can keep the conversation short and to the point.

You will now have to learn how to function in society. In spite of all the negative aspects of your upbringing, it has taught you some valuable skills: you are capable of adjusting to others; you are trained at doing domestic chores. You have also learned to survive under difficult circumstances and are used to the fact that things often do not go your way. Unlike many men, you are not spoiled. But there is still much that you can learn: do not resist making the effort. It will be worth it.

FOURTEEN

Submission:

Part I

This is a transcript of the original document that I took to Theo van Gogh, which he read and proposed that we make into a movie. It was first broadcast on Dutch television in August 2004. On November 2, 2004, Theo van Gogh was murdered on the streets of Amsterdam.

Submission is about God and the individual. I did not write this script to provoke anyone. As I mentioned in the preface of this book, I wrote it to show the abolutism with which the individual Muslim woman is expected to totally submit herself to God's will and God's word as written in the Koran. I wanted to introduce a shift in the relationship between the individual and God, and I wanted this shift to move us from a relationship of total submission to one of dialogue. I chose the structure of the prayer because Muslims are supposed to pray five times a day. That's why there are five different women praying in five different ways. The sense of the film is of these faithful women who have submitted themselves to God's will and who are continuing to pray under terrible circumstances as they try to elicit a response from God. They are saying, Look, God, I've submitted completely to you, but everything is going wrong. Yet, you, God, remain silent.

This transcript is called *Part I* because I *will* write more parts. Again, I will not do this out of any desire to insult or provoke. But I feel that reasonable people and reasonable people of faith must confront Allah with the dilemmas He places us in and requires us to face on earth. Our dilemmas—the dilemmas that men and women face every day—arise directly out of His commands.

Part II will be about four men who have trouble following God's commands and, like the women of *Part I*, confront God during prayer with their demands.

In *Part III*, God will answer.

1. INTRODUCTION

Amina is a dedicated Muslim woman who dutifully adheres to the rules of the Shari'a. She is surrounded by women who are treated cruelly in the name of Allah: they suffer abuse, marital rape, incest, and corporal punishment. These acts of cruelty are justified by verses from the Koran. Amina feels sorry for the victims and identifies with their fate. Every day she turns to Allah and prays fervently for an improvement in their circumstances, but Allah remains silent and the cruelties continue.

One day Amina does something surprising. She does not adhere to the fixed routine of the prayer ritual. After reading the compulsory opening chapter to the Koran she launches into a spontaneous "dialogue" with Allah, instead of subjecting herself to him.

Location: Islamistan [an imaginary country where the majority of the population is Muslim, and where the legal system is the Shari'a].

CAST

Amina: main character (addressing Allah in prayer)

Aisha: curled up in fetal position recovering from the pain caused by one hundred strokes of the cane

Safiya: her experience of sexual intercourse with her husband is as rape

Zainab: severely bruised, having been beaten up by her husband, who considers her disobedient

Fatima: wearing a veil, a victim of incest

The five women take up their positions. Amina sits at the center, her head bowed. She gets up, walks over to a prayer rug in front of her, and unrolls it. The rug points in the direction of Mecca. Amina stands at the end of the rug; she faces Mecca. She raises her arms up into the air, with her palms exposed, and shouts "Allahu Akbar." Then she folds her arms across her chest and places her right hand over her left. Finally she fixes her gaze on the opposite end of the prayer rug. She remains in this position until the *Sura Fatiha* [The Opening] has been read. When she hears "Aaaammiiin," she merely lifts up her head and stares into the camera.

1. AISHA, WHO HAS BEEN SENTENCED TO ONE HUNDRED STROKES OF THE CANE.

Amina delivers the speech below, which tells the fate of a woman called Aisha. Meanwhile, the camera slowly moves from Amina to Aisha. Aisha is lying on the floor in the fetal position. The wounds (scars) on her body, caused by the strokes of the cane, are visible. Written across them is text from the Koran: chapter 24, verse 2 (Al-Nur, or The Light).

Amina's Speech

O Allah, as I lie here wounded, my spirit broken
I hear in my head the judge's voice as he pronounces me guilty.
The sentence I have to serve is in your words:
*"The woman and the man guilty of adultery or fornication
flog each of them with a hundred stripes;*

let no compassion move you in their case, in a matter prescribed by God,
if ye believe in God and the Last Day; and let a party of the believers
    witness their
punishment."* [This quotation in italics is written across Aisha's
    body.]

Two years ago, on a sunny day, while in the *souk* my eyes were
    caught by those of
Rahman, the most handsome man I have ever met.
After that day, I couldn't help but notice his presence whenever I
    went to the marketplace.
I was thrilled when I learned that his appearance in the bazaar
    was not a coincidence.
One day he suggested we meet in secret, and I said, "Yes."
For months Rahman and I met, shared drinks and delicacies.
We danced and dreamed . . . yeah, we built beautiful castles in the
    air.
And we made love, on every secret meeting.
As the months went by our relationship deepened.
What is more, out of our love a new life started to grow.
Our happiness did not go unnoticed and before long, envious eyes
    gave way to malicious tongues.
"Let's ignore these people and trust in Allah's mercy." Rahman and
    I said to each other.
Naïve, young, and in love perhaps, but we thought that Your
    holiness was on our side.
Rahman and I shared affection, trust, and a deep respect for each
    other; how can God disapprove? Why would He?

And so we ignored the mean tongues, and together we continued
    to live our dream, albeit in more secrecy.
O, Allah, until we were summoned to court and charged with
    fornication!

Rahman called me a day before we were to appear before the judge.

He said that his father had smuggled him out of the country. What a pity that my father happens to be a pious man, I thought.

Rahman told me that he loved me and that he would pray for me. He also encouraged me to be strong and have faith in you.

O Allah, how can I have faith in you? You who reduced my love to fornication?

I lie here flogged—abused and shamed—in your name.

The verdict that killed my faith in love is in your holy book.

Faith in you, submission to you, feels like—*is*—self-betrayal.

2. SAFIYA, WHO IS SYSTEMATICALLY RAPED BY HER HUSBAND

Amina delivers the speech below, which tells the fate of an imaginary woman called Safiya. Meanwhile, the camera slowly turns from Amina to Safiya. We get a view of a beautiful woman from behind; she is wearing a full-length white robe with a low-cut back. Written across her back and thighs (the robe has a split at the front) we see the text from the Koran: chapter 2, verse 222 (Al-Baqara, or The Cow).

Amina's Speech

When I was sixteen my father broke the news to me in the kitchen.

"You are going to marry Azziz; he is from a virtuous family, and he will take good care of you."

When I saw pictures of Azziz, instead of feeling excitement I thought of him as unattractive, and even though I did my best to see the perfect whole,

I couldn't help but notice his faulty details:

a scar on the lip, a bent nose, so much hair on the eyebrows.

My wedding day was more my family's celebration than mine.
Once in my marital home my husband approached me.
Ever since then I recoil from his touch.
I am repulsed by his smell, even if he has just had a bath,
Yet, O Allah, I obey his command
Sanctioned by your words.
I let him take me.
Each time I push him away he quotes you:
"They ask thee
concerning women's courses
Say: they are a hurt and a pollution
So keep away from women
In their courses, and do not
Approach them until
They are clean.
But when they have
Purified themselves,
Ye may approach them in any manner, time, or place
Ordained for you by God.
For God loves those
Who turn to Him constantly
And He loves those who keep themselves pure and clean."
So I stretch the days of my period,
But of course there comes a time when I must
Undress. He orders me and I submit
Not to him, but to you.
Lately, enduring my husband is getting harder and harder.
O, Allah, I pray, give me the strength to endure him or I fear
My faith shall weaken.

3. ZAINAB, WHO IS BEATEN BY HER HUSBAND

Amina delivers the speech below, which tells the fate of a woman
called Zainab. Meanwhile, the camera slowly moves from Amina to

Zainab. We see Zainab's swollen face, which is covered in bruises. Her clothes have been ripped from her body. Written across the exposed parts of her body—her upper arms, shoulders and, possibly, her stomach—we see the text from the Koran: chapter 4, verse 34 (Al-Nisa, or The Women).

Amina's Speech

O Allah, most high,
You say that *"Men are the protectors and maintainers of women,*
    because you have given the one more (strength) than the other."
I feel, at least once a week the strength of my husband's fist on my
    face,
O Allah, most high,
Life with my husband is hard to bear,
But I submit my will to you.
My husband supports me from his means,
Therefore, I am devoutly obedient, and I guard in my husband's
    absence what you would have me guard. But my husband,
    maintainer and protector, fears disloyalty and
ill conduct on my part; he accuses me of being ungrateful to him.
Like an army general on the battlefield he screams his every whim
    at me;
Threatens never to share my bed again,
And goes away for nights on end.
I suspect to another woman.
I dare not ask him about her
Even though family and friends whisper about him and the other
    woman.
When he comes back
He always finds a reason to doubt my loyalty to him,
And after a series of warnings and threats he starts to beat me.
First lightly on my arms and legs, just as you, most high describe—
    ahhhuh O shall I say prescribe—in your holy book;

But mostly on the face.
And why?
For not responding fast enough to his orders,
For ironing the wrong shirt,
For not putting enough salt in the food,
For chatting too long with my sister on the phone.

O, God, most elevated, submission to your will assures me of a
      better life in the hereafter,
But I feel that the price I pay for my husband's protection and
      maintenance is too high.
I wonder how much longer I will submit.

4. FATIMA, THE VEILED WOMAN

Amina delivers the speech below, which tells the fate of a woman
called Fatima. Meanwhile, the camera slowly moves from Amina to
Fatima. We see a woman veiled from head to toe; a lattice of
threads dangling in front of her eyes suggests she is peering through
a barred window. She is sitting down, and the draperies of her robe
reveal her feminine contours. Printed across the veil, in white ink,
are the texts from the Koran: chapter 24, verse 31 (Al-Nur, or The
Light).

Amina's Speech

O Allah, most gracious, most merciful.
Just as you demand of the believing woman, I lower my gaze and
      guard my modesty.
I never display my beauty and ornaments; not even my face or
      hands.
I never strike with my feet in order to draw attention to my hidden
      ornaments, not even at parties.
I never go out of the house unless it is absolutely necessary; and

then only with my father's permission. When I do go out I draw
my veil over my bosom as you wish.

Once in a while I sin. I fantasize about feeling the wind through
my hair or the sun on my skin, perhaps on the beach. I
daydream about an extended journey through the world,
imagining all the places and peoples out there. Of course, I shall
never see these places or meet many people because it is so
important to guard my modesty in order to please you, O Allah.
So I cheerfully do as you say and cover my body from head to
toe except while I am in the house and with family members
only. In general I am happy with my life.

However, since my father's brother Hakim is staying with us
Things have changed!
Hakim waits till I am alone at home and comes to my room.
Then he orders me to do things to him, touch him in places most
intimate.
Since he is with us I took to the habit of wearing the veil inside the
house in order to deter him. That doesn't stop him, though.
Twice now he unveiled me, ripped my inner garments, and raped
me.
When I told my mother she said she would take it up with my
father.
My father ordered her—and me—not to question his brother's
honor.

I experience pain each time my uncle comes to see me.
I feel caged, like an animal waiting for slaughter.
I am filled with guilt and shame;
and I feel abandoned, yet I am surrounded by family and friends.
O Allah, Hakim is gone, now that he knows I am pregnant.
For the moment I can hide my abdomen behind my veil, but
sooner or later someone will notice. I shall be openly shamed

and killed by my father for not being a virgin.

When I consider this, I think of taking my life but know that in the
hereafter the one who commits suicide shall never count on
your mercy.
O Allah, giver and taker of life.
You admonish all who believe to turn toward you in order to attain
bliss.
I have done nothing my whole life but turn to you.
And now that I pray for salvation, under my veil, you remain silent
as the grave I long for.
I wonder how much longer I am able to submit!

FIFTEEN

The Need for Self-Reflection Within Islam

[This is Ayaan's answer to a critical reaction to *Submission: Part I,* that was published in *De Volkskrant.*]

My parents brought me up with the idea that Islam is the most beautiful way of life—morally, socially, and spiritually. Years later I realized that there are ugly blemishes that spoil the beauty of Islam. These imperfections, however, are invisible to those who share my parents' religious convictions and who justify the wrongs of Islam by repeating over and over that it is not that the religion is at fault, but the faithful who have made a mess of things.

Islamic morality demands that the individual subject himself completely to the will of Allah through the Shari'a, the code of law derived from the Koran, and to the religious community. The Muslim as an individual can do nothing individually: he even has to sit, eat, sleep, and travel according to strict rules; he cannot freely choose his own friends and is expected to have (and avoid) certain thoughts and feelings. Anything that has not been covered by Allah and His Prophet becomes the domain of the religious community, which comprises the immediate family to the worldwide Muslim community. For example: if a Moroccan Muslim were to behave improperly after a few beers, it would be fine for a person from, say,

Sudan or Afghanistan to call him to order—in the absence of other Moroccans—for no other reason than that this bystander happened to be a fellow Muslim.

Nowhere is the denial of Muslim individuality felt more strongly than in the relationship between the sexes. Islamic sexual morality places a heavy emphasis on chastity. Sex is only allowed in a marital context. In practice this puts more of a restriction on women than on men. It is all right for men, for example, to marry four wives, but not the other way around. The position of Muslim women, compared to that of many of their non-Islamic sisters, is, frankly, bad—they are powerless, subjugated, unequal.

Like the rest of the world, however, Muslims take advantage of modern scientific progress. Those who can afford to do so make extensive use of technological developments, such as cars and airplanes. They live in modern buildings and work with machines and computers. However, the moral framework of Islam, unlike that of Christianity and Judaism, has not changed with the times. Every Muslim, from the beginnings of Islam to the present day, is raised in the belief that all knowledge can be found in the Koran, that it is wrong to ask critical questions, and that every Muslim (even in 2004) should strive to imitate the life of Islam's founder Muhammad. In practice, of course, few manage to organize their lives in perfect agreement with the principles of the seventh-century prophet.

As a result of this restrictive upbringing, basic human curiosity in Muslims has been seriously curtailed. Any new step a Muslim dares to take will be rejected by the rest of the community on the grounds that it is unfamiliar and not in line with the Koran. Islam is a static faith.

After the events of 9/11, people who deny this characterization of the stagnant state of Islam were challenged by critical outsiders to name a single Muslim who had made a discovery in science or technology, or changed the world through artistic achievement. There is none. In a community of over 1.2 billion faithful, knowledge, progress, and prosperity are not primary aspirations. Poverty, violence, and decline are widespread. To reverse this situation, we need to change the moral framework of Muslim upbringing.

It is in the interests of Muslims themselves to open a critical discussion about Islam, but it is also crucial to the rest of the world. Almost all current political conflicts involve Muslims. The majority of Muslims live in dire circumstances: starvation, disease, overpopulation, and unemployment are widespread. In their native countries, Muslims are the victims of oppressive regimes, which are usually based on the Shari'a. Most Muslims have no access to any education of reasonable quality; many are illiterate. It can no longer be denied that Muslims themselves are often (without meaning to) responsible for this misery. A thorough analysis of Islam and the amendment of a great many Islamic dogmas, which presently keep the faithful trapped in a cycle of violence and poverty, would give Muslims the chance to end individual oppression and to achieve a sexual morality in which men, women, and homosexuals are treated as equals.

This critical appreciation will have to come from within, from the very people who were raised in the Islamic tradition but who were not blinded to the flaws that undermine the beauty of their culture—people who have had a decent education and the chance to meet people outside the Muslim community. These people have pursued their individual happiness and know how difficult it is to combine being a good Muslim with following the human inner need for freedom. They live in free countries and can openly declare their views without immediately feeling their lives are in danger. Nonetheless, these critics of Islam will have to understand that a culture that dates back many centuries and has never been through a period of self-reflection is not going to welcome their insights. They will be regarded, as other dissenters have been, as traitors and deserters who foul their own nests.

How exactly should this Muslim self-reflection be expressed? I believe that every form of self-expression should be allowed, except for physical and verbal abuse. Use words (novels, nonfiction, poetry, cartoons), images (film, animations, paintings, and other art forms), and sound. *Submission: Part I,* the short film I made with Theo van Gogh, expresses my aspiration to question the morality central to my upbringing. I do not aim to transform Muslims into atheists, but I do want to expose the blemishes of the culture, particularly its cruel treatment of women. I have observed firsthand the undeniable connection between the rules of the Koran, which state that a disobedient wife should be beaten, and the violent practice of wife beating. The account of this practice is in the *hadiths* (sayings attributed to the Prophet Muhammad), and violent Muslim men quote from the Koran whenever anyone confronts them about their behavior in everyday life. Even the victims of physical abuse themselves cite the Koran to justify the violent actions of the men, and often return to their husbands, promising they will be more obedient and improve their behavior in the future. So, on top of their physical suffering, these victims are so brainwashed that they "willingly" subject themselves to the very doctrine that is at the root of their deplorable circumstances.

When *Submission: Part I* was shown as part of the television series *Zomergasten* [*Summer Guests*] it sparked many critical reactions. Many people were pleased to see the oppression of Muslim women confronted, although they questioned the effectiveness of the strategy I had chosen. One group, which includes the Amsterdam historian Lucassen, thinks that criticism of the shadowy aspects of Islam is unnecessary doom mongering. They believe critics of Islam are unnecessarily pessimistic and give the example of third-generation Muslims who no longer spend most of their day in the mosques and whose daughters happily combine headscarves with cropped tops. They believe that this evolution will continue without the need for criticism.

I am not a defeatist. I am an optimist. But a critical approach will humanize Islam, and it is necessary. Lucassen and his cronies confuse those who follow the faith with the faith itself. Islam is a way of life, a system of ideas. Every believer is taught to accept the system as immutable, unshakeable. By pointing out that a merciful God who authorizes the abuse of women is inconsistent, I force Muslims to face a shortcoming in their faith and to discover the meaning and importance of secular morality, which will enable them to adapt their faith to the real world. Criticism of Islam does not mean that the faithful reject it. But it does mean that the faithful examine particular ideas and teaching that, when applied in real life, lead to brutal behavior with unacceptable consequences.

Others warned me, after seeing *Submission,* that my criticism of Islam was counterproductive, that Islamophobes would be eager to use my views to discriminate against Muslims and to place Islam in an evil light. This may be true, but it was never my intention to play into the hands of Islamophobes. My intention was to challenge Muslims, through thought-provoking texts and images, to think carefully about the extent of their own responsibility for their deprived circumstances. The risk that Islamophobes or racists will misuse my work will not stop me from making *Submission: Part II.* A journalist who rightly demands openness of affairs in a liberal democracy (think of Guantánamo Bay), is not going to let himself be stopped by the government's fear that providing that information could be used by the enemies of the free world. I have to make the same type of decision as journalists and champions of civil rights. Exposing the wrongs of the world (including religious wrongs) outweighs the possible risk of misuse by third parties.

Some of my critics said that Muslims would be offended and troubled by a film like *Submission* and would only dig their heels deeper into the sand, resisting change. They also believed that my confrontational methods would be counterproductive, and that I should modify my strategy. Typically, this group of critics, which includes the Muslim Labor Representatives Arib and Al-Bayrak, fails to offer a more effective, alternate strategy. They concentrate too much on the pain felt by smooth talkers such as the Arab-European League leaders and people like Mr. Ayhan Tonca, chairman of the

Contact Group for Muslims and Government, but ignore the extreme, continuing, daily pain of the victims of violence. Yet these Islamic "social democrats" would rather defend and preserve a doctrine that subjugates women than attempt to enlighten people.

They do not want change—and they do not want a light shone on the ugly results of their "faith." They turn their eyes away from a Muslim woman who, at the age of twenty-three, cannot read or write and spends her days curled up in the corner of a shelter for abused women. Less than three years ago this woman was snatched from her family in the remote countryside of a Muslim state and found herself living in an apartment in a squalid housing development in a big city, sharing her life with a stranger she had been forced to marry. When this man began to beat her regularly, the police moved her to the women's shelter. There, she sits listlessly in a corner, passively watching her baby crawl around restlessly. She barely responds to the irritated looks of the other women or the repeated reminders from members of staff that she must take care of her child. This woman is homeless. She can no longer return to her family in her native country because she has become the property of her husband. When I question her about her own and her child's future, she answers that her faith is in Allah: "Through Allah I ended up in these circumstances, and if I am patient He will get me out of this misery. I only have to obey Him." In *Submission: Part I*, I try to show how this kind of submission to Allah works out in real life.

Yet the Al-Nisa organization of Muslim women believes that since 9/11 Muslims have come under heavy pressure. They feel pushed into a corner, unfairly held responsible for the actions of people who are up to nasty things in faraway countries and call themselves Muslims. The organization's chair thinks that criticism of the position of Muslim women is in itself a good thing, but that my timing in making the movie was unfortunate and that Muslims must not be hurt.

This argument is incorrect. Muslims in the Netherlands are not cornered. On the contrary, they fully enjoy the freedom of religion that prevails in this Western secular country and its enormous prosperity. The fact is: as long as Muslims here are not in charge of the country, they will go on feeling hurt.

Many Muslims react with outrage when flaws in their religion are pointed out to them. Some threaten physical violence, or become verbally abusive. Here are comments about *Submission; Part I* from some official spokespeople for Dutch Muslim organizations (although nobody knows exactly who they represent):

"Hirsi Ali's film defeats the object. Discussing the position of women in Islam is a good thing. But this is a terrible shock for devout Muslims, many of whom will immediately feel the need to become defensive. This spoils the debate in the Netherlands. Right now it would be better if we focused on restoring a normal relationship. I have no idea what her motives were, but I regard it as pure provocation." These are the words of Mohamed Sini, chairman of the Trust for Islam and Citizenship, who says he respects, above all, the freedom of speech.

The chairman of the Netherlands branch of the Arab-European League (AEL) says: "The discussion about the position of Islam is weakened by Hirsi Ali's confrontation. It comes as no surprise that Theo van Gogh does this sort of thing; he never has a constructive thought about anything. But she is a member of the Dutch House of Representatives. I cannot think why she wants to offend millions of Muslims in the Netherlands." He says that—except for some extreme cases—there is little wrong with the position of women in the Islamic world. "Dutch people who would like to find out a little more about this should not listen to Hirsi Ali only. She projects her own bizarre experiences onto the whole group."

Having ranted on like this, he then admits that he never even saw the film: "I'm not going to waste my time on this madness."

Just before the film was broadcast on television, a spokesperson for the Contact Group for Muslims and Government commented, "I am not in the least bit interested in that little film, and I don't want to see it. It will be a distortion of the facts, anyway. I find it absurd that Hirsi Ali does nothing but provoke. It's time for her to keep her mouth shut." He chooses to "ignore" Hirsi Ali and Van Gogh completely: "That is the best strategy; sooner or later they'll stop. They simply don't deserve a reaction."

The chairman of the Turkish Muslim organization Milli Görüs said, in the Rotterdam daily, "If Hirsi Ali wants to wage a religious war, that is her business; I have decided not to comment on it [the film]."

The chairman of the Netherlands Muslim Council responded to *Submission:* "For the Islamic community this is one step too far. The more orthodox Muslims will certainly not accept this."

Driss El Boujoufi of the Union of Moroccan Muslim Organizations in the Netherlands (UMMON) had the following to say: "Ayaan Hirsi Ali wants it to be a competition, and she is looking for opponents. But we're not playing her game, because as soon as it becomes a contest, you attract spectators, and that is the last thing we want."

A spokesperson for the Netherlands Muslim Broadcasting Network says: "Hirsi Ali has a problem with these verses from the Koran. But it is not the Koran that incites men to abuse women, it is the men themselves. She should address them directly and invite them to discuss the matter. Emancipation begins from within. If you attack what people value, you will lose their trust."

All these reactions were fairly predictable. It does not matter whether the person commenting has actually seen *Submission.* It does not matter whether the critical reflections on Islam are expressed in the form of a short film, a text, or something else. These people just want to deny Islam's biggest weakness: the way in which women are regarded and treated. Leaders of Muslim organizations warn that the Muslim community will not accept the images of women whose bodies have been painted with verses from the Koran. But the fact is that Muslim organizations, and Muslims in general, have for centuries gone along with what actually happens when the message contained in these verses is applied to the bodies of the actresses in *Submission:* the lashing of "unchaste" women, the systematic mistreatment of "disobedient" women, the rape of married women by permission of Allah, and the ostracizing, or even murder, of girls and women who have become the victims of incest. All this is followed slavishly, thoughtlessly to clear the family name of shame.

Representatives of Muslim organizations deny the message contained in *Submission* and also deny the fact that large groups of Muslim women are forced to take refuge in women's shelters, that many are dumped by their husbands in their country of origin, with all their children and no money. The Department of Justice has actually been stopped from keeping a systematic record of the number of honor killings that occur each year, because sophistic spokespeople for Muslim organizations warn that this would upset the people whose interests they protect. Yet the regional institutes for mental welfare and other mental health care services are aware that many Muslim girls become the victims of incest and forced marriages and are taken away by their fathers to be murdered in the family's country of origin. Whose interests are being protected by the government here? Murderers are being protected.

The hidden agenda of the conservative spokespeople of Muslim organizations is the same as the agenda of Muslim schools: Western Muslims want to be free to decide how they treat the female members of their family. These are organized enemies of women, and they endorse the unspoken consensus that prevails in Islamic countries: how women and girls are treated is a private family matter. If any female behavior seems remotely threatening to the family honor, then fathers, brothers, and any other male relatives may intervene as they think fit. Verses in the Koran are used to justify male violence against women, and also to appease the perpetrator's conscience and that of any witnesses. By exempting the holy text from all criticism, the leaders of Muslim organizations everywhere successfully preserve the system that underlies the oppression of women. And so they perpetuate its practice.

In fact, the majority of Muslim men do not regard the way they treat women as "oppressive," "abusive," or "murderous"; they feel that violence is a fair response to the way women behave. As one Muslim spokesperson said, "Muslim women know the rules. If they choose to overstep the mark, they will be punished," and "with the exception of some extreme cases, there is little wrong with the position of women in the Islamic world." Doesn't that speak volumes?

Yet Muslims think I place too much emphasis on the negative aspects of Islam. They ask why I do not make a fuss about the intolerance among Christians or Jews and believe that I am more interested in putting Islam in a bad light than in improving the position of women.

It is true that the Bible and the Talmud also contain passages that reflect hostility toward women. And, yes indeed, there are Christians and Jews who interpret those holy texts in the same literal vein as many Muslims do when studying the Koran. Some of these people are in the grip of a sexual morality that is indistinguishable from that of Shari'a countries like Saudi Arabia. They treat women just as badly, resist all progress, and are intolerant of homosexuals.

But if these critical Muslims took their comparative analysis a little further, they would discover that the number of "word nazis" in the Christian and Jewish worlds is far smaller than in the Islamic world. The God of the Christians and Jews has been tamed by reasonable people and largely moved to the believer's private conscience. Nowadays, God is referred to as "love" or as "energy," and those who believe in Him have done away with the concept of hell. Christianity and Judaism have lost their grip on the individual, although the priests, ministers, and rabbis have not allowed this to happen of their own free will. The prevalence of freedom of conscience, the search for knowledge, and the individual control over human nature in the West were hard-won conquests, all of which began as a battle of words.

Most women born in what were originally Jewish-Christian states can safely go out in the streets on their own, have equal access to education, reap the rewards of their labor, and choose with whom they want to share their lives. They are in charge of their sexual needs, the decision to get pregnant, and the number of children they want. Most of the women of Jewish or Christian descent are free to travel around the world, buy a house of their own, and have their own possessions. Not all of them, but the majority. Only a tiny fraction of the women in Muslim families can do any of these things. They have virtually no right of self-determination.

Jews and Christians have achieved this in the West by criticizing their holy texts, by ridiculing things that are said in the Bible and Talmud, and pointing out that many of these things are wrong. The ancient texts have survived, but our ideas about how the sexes should relate to each other have moved on. When Jews and Christians discovered the power of words and images, they used them to shine a light onto their belief and culture, to find inconsistencies, to stop harmful practices, and to promote merciful, humane ones. Time after time, those who wanted to preserve the status quo complained that the texts, images, and behavior of their critics were "hurtful," "sinful," and "radical." For centuries the church encouraged the faithful to ignore its critics. It held inquisitions. It ignored priests who behaved immorally and illegally until the people would not allow it anymore. The same must happen in Islam. The people who truly love the beauty of their faith must act to stamp out the ugliness.

The history of the West is the search for enlightenment through self-reflection. This is the source of its democratic practices and its power. I have borrowed my strategy of criticizing Islam from the Jewish-Christian insurrection against the absolutism of religious faith. I made *Submission: Part I* in this context. How effective my controversial strategy can be will be known to anyone familiar with the struggle between the churches of the West. As I say, I am an optimist.

SIXTEEN

Portrait of a Heroine
as a Young Woman

One of my current heroines is Samira Ahmed, a twenty-four-year-old girlishly pretty woman with large, brown, doelike eyes, dark, curly hair, and a smile that seduces even the gloomiest of faces to lighten up and smile back. Besides her good nature, she is also inquisitive and has a strong will to be her own person. Born to a family who left Morocco in the early 1980s and settled in the Netherlands, she is one of ten children.

In the summer of 2005, I attended her graduation ceremony at a training college in Amsterdam. Samira received a diploma for pedagogy and a record 10 score (the highest score possible) for her thesis.

This is the celebratory side of Samira's story, for there is also a tragic side. When I arrived for Samira's graduation I was received like all the other guests in a reception area just outside of the auditorium where the ceremony was to take place. I noticed the happy class, a total of thirty-five students, gathered in clusters around coffee stands. Family and friends accompanied them, chatting, carrying gifts and flowers wrapped in cellophane. Proud fathers and mothers, flushed siblings teasing their red-faced brothers and sisters, boyfriends and girlfriends happy just to be there to witness an achiever in the family.

On Samira's stand none of her family showed up: no brother, no sister, no cousin, no nephew, no niece.

Two years earlier, Samira had had to sneak away from home because she wanted to live in a students' house like her Dutch friends Sara and Marloes. At home she had shared a bedroom with some of her siblings and had no privacy at all. Every move she made in the house was monitored by her mother and sisters; outside the house her brothers kept watch. They all wanted to make sure that under no circumstances would she become Westernized.

Samira had endured terrible physical and psychological violence at home. Her family always had a pretext to question her, go through her stuff, and forbid her from setting foot outside the house. She was beaten frequently. There were rumors in her community that she had a Dutch boyfriend. The beatings at home became harsher. Samira could bear it no longer and left. Soon afterward, in the summer of 2003, she got in touch with me. I went with her to the police to file a complaint against her brothers, who had threatened to murder her. According to them, Samira's death was the only way to avenge the shame she brought upon the family for leaving their parents' house. The police said they could do nothing to help her except file the complaint. They said there were thousands of other women like her and it was not the police's duty to intervene in family matters.

Ever since she left, Samira has been in hiding, moving from house to house and depending on the kindness of strangers. Mostly she is brave and faces life with a powerful optimism. Samira reads her textbooks, does her homework, and turns her papers in on time. She accepts invitations to student parties from Sara and Marloes and makes an effort to enjoy herself. Sometimes, however, she has a sad, drawn look on her face that betrays her worries. Once in a while she just weeps and confides that she wishes her life were different, perhaps more like the lives of her Dutch friends.

Today, however, on her graduation day, she is glowing, clutching her diploma and returning the kisses of her friends. Her worries are far from over, though. She has no money; she has to find a job, and with her Moroccan name that will be far from easy in the Netherlands; she has to find another new place to live; she lives in an unending fear of being discovered by her brothers and slaughtered by them. This is no joke, for in just two police regions in Holland (The Hague area and the southern section of the province of South Holland) eleven Muslim girls were killed by their own families between October 2004 and May 2005 for "offenses" similar to those committed by Samira.

AS A SPOKESPERSON for immigrants in Dutch society, I regularly advocate the emancipation of immigrant women. In my mind, there are three categories of Muslim women in Dutch society. I suspect that this distinction applies to other European Union countries with large Muslim populations as well.

First, there are girls like Samira—strong-willed, intelligent, and willing to take a chance on shaping their individual futures along a path they choose for themselves. They face many obstacles as they try to assimilate in Western society and some may lose their lives trying to attain their dreams.

Second, there are girls and women who are very dependent and attached to their families but who cleverly forge a way to lead a double life. Instead of confronting their families and arguing about their adherence to custom and religion, these girls use a more tactful approach. When with family (in the broadest sense of the word, which also includes their community), they put on their headscarves and at home obey every whim of their parents and menfolk. Outside the home, however, they lead the life of an average Western woman: they have a job, dress fashionably, have a boyfriend, drink alcohol, attend cocktail parties, and even manage to travel away from home for a while.

The third group are the utterly vulnerable. Some of these girls are imported as brides or domestic workers from the country of origin of the immigrants with whom they come to live. Some are daughters of the more conservative families. These girls are removed from school once they attain puberty and locked up at home. Their families get away with this form of modern slavery because the authorities rarely take notice of these young women. The girls have often been brought up to be absolutely obedient; they perform household chores without question. Their individual wills have been bent to the servitude taught at their parents' house and put into practice in their husbands' homes or the homes of the people who import and enslave them. They can hardly read or write. When they marry, they generally bear as many children as their individual fertility allows. When they miscarry, most of them view this as God's will, not as a lack of proper health care, which they are usually prevented from seeking because of their families' religious reasons.

When a woman in this subjugated state is violently abused by husband, brother, or father, she considers it a result of her own wrongdoing. In response, she promises to behave better in the future. Some abused women may be tempted to rebel by running away or informing the authorities when their life becomes too painful. Those who act on such a temptation are likely to be killed by their own family or husband, or end up in prostitution or in the women's shelters. Some who have shown signs of rebellion are lured back to their country of origin by parents or husbands and simply dumped there, abandoned, disowned, with or without children, and with no financial resources or people to help them.

For a while now I have been asserting that the most effective way for European Union governments to deal with their Muslim minorities is to empower the Muslim women living within their borders. No one has offered a convincing argument against this position, but no one outside my own party seems to want to make the first step to help these women. The best tool for empowering these women is education. Yet the education systems of some European Union countries are going through a crisis of neglect, particularly with regard to immigrant children. We are now paying the price of mixing education with ideology. However, let me stick to the important subject of freeing women from the shackles of superstitious belief and tribal custom.

The biggest obstacle that hinders Muslim women from leading dignified, free lives is violence—physical, mental, and sexual—committed by their close families. Here is only a sample of some of the violence perpetrated on girls and women from Islamic cultures:

- Four-year-old girls have their genitals mutilated: some of them so badly that they die of infections; others are traumatized for life from the experience and will later suffer recurrent infections of their reproductive and urinary systems.

- Teenage girls are removed from school by force and kept inside the house to stop their schooling, stifle their thinking, and suffocate their will.

- Victims of incest and sexual abuse are beaten, deported, or killed to prevent them from filing complaints.

- Some pregnant victims of incest or abuse are forced to have abortions by their fathers, older brothers, or uncles in order to keep the family honor from being stained. In this era of DNA testing, the girls could demonstrate that they have been abused. Yet instead of punishing the abusers, the family treats the daughter as if she had dishonored the family.

- Girls and women who protest their maltreatment are beaten by their parents in order to kill their spirits and reduce them to a lifelong servitude that amounts to slavery.

- Many girls and women who can't bear to suffer anymore take their own lives or develop numerous kinds of psychological ailments, including nervous breakdown and psychosis. They are literally driven mad.

- A Muslim girl in Europe runs more of a risk than girls of other faiths of being forced into marriage by her parents with a stranger. In such a marriage—which, since it is forced, by definition starts with rape—she conceives child after child. She is an enslaved womb. Many of her children will grow up in a household with parents who are neither bound by love nor interested in the well-being of their children. The daughters will go through life as subjugated as their mothers and the sons become—in Europe—dropouts from school, attracted to pastimes that can vary from loitering in the streets to drug abuse to radical Islamic fundamentalism.

European policy makers have not yet understood the huge potential of liberating Muslim women. They are squandering the single best opportunity they have to make Muslim integration a success within one generation.

Morally, governments need to eradicate violence against women in Europe. This would make clear to fundamentalists that Europeans take their constitutions seriously. Now, most abusers simply think that Western rhetoric about the equality of men and women is cowardly and hypocritical, since Western governments tolerate the abuse of millions of Muslim women when they're told it's in the name of freedom of religion.

Muslim women like Samira would make sure to prepare their own children for a life in modern society. These women would plan their family with a chosen partner. This planning reduces the chances for dropouts among their children. They value education and would emphasize its importance for their children. They value work and aspire to make contribution to the economy. They would provide the graying European economy with the human resources it needs instead of adding to its social welfare rolls.

The children of successful Muslim women are more likely to have a positive attitude toward the societies in which they live. They will learn at an early age to appreciate the freedom and prosperity they live in and perhaps even understand how vulnerable these freedoms are and defend them.

WHY ARE EUROPEAN leaders so slow to appreciate the great role Muslim women can play in a successful integration of immigrants in the European Union? Some blame can be attributed to the passivity of universities and nongovernmental organizations in addressing immigrant women's rights. The academic community unanimously condemns violence against women, whether it is committed by family or the state, but it has been negligent in investigating and providing the necessary legal framework and data to help policy makers make women's rights a priority. The classic argument of professors that universities are not political arenas seems disingenuous, since many faculties and colleges across Europe indulge in all sorts of ideological and political practices. For instance, Oxford University has just given a chair to Tariq Ramadan, the Swiss Muslim ideologist seen by some as a moderate voice propounding the assimilation of Muslims into European society by "psychological integration" and by some Americans and Europeans as a radical. He was hired in the summer of 2005 by the University of Notre Dame in the United States to teach Islamic philosophy and ethics at its Joan B. Kroc Institute for Peace & Justice, but he was denied entry into the country, his visa revoked just days before he was to begin working there. Ultimately, he resigned from the post, since he could not get there to teach. His hiring by Oxford appears to be not solely because of his outstanding academic record but because he is seen as buffer against radical Islam.

Yet, in spite of having Arab and Islam faculties, most universities in Europe serve as activist centers to further the Palestinian cause, instead of research and teaching centers for Muslim students. There is as yet no chair, no study, no course on the subjugation of Muslim women and how that affects Europe and the future of this major population of European Muslims. There are no researchers gathering facts and figures on the intensity of violence faced by Muslim women, how that violence hinders them in their daily lives, and how that prevents Muslims from integrating successfully into European society.

Nongovernmental organizations are embarrassingly silent on this fight for human rights. Oh, yes, there is one in Norway that pays attention, Human Rights Watch, run by a brave, determined woman, Hege Storhaus. But in the bigger countries, no NGO yet monitors the number of times an honor killing is committed in a member state, or the number of times a girl is circumcised, or the number of times a girl is removed from school and forced into a life of virtual slavery.

However, there is room for some optimism. Awareness is growing in Europe about the breadth and persistence of violence against Muslim women and girls, justified by culture and religion, committed by family. Some governments have acknowledged that they should take action to fight against this and all types of violence against women. Yet we are a long way away from conditions where girls like Samira can lead a life without fear.

What a waste that Europe is blind to this golden opportunity that lies at her feet.

SEVENTEEN

A Call for Clear Thinking

After the carnage of the terrorist bombings in London on July 7, 2005, Tony Blair defined the situation as a battle of ideas. "Our values will long outlast theirs," he said, to the silent acquiescence of the world leaders who stood alongside him. "Whatever [the terrorists] do, it is our determination that they will never succeed in destroying what we hold dear in this country and in other civilized nations throughout the world."

By defining this as a battle of values, Blair raised the question, Which values are at stake? Those who love freedom know that the open society relies on a few key shared concepts. They believe that all humans are born free, are endowed with reason, and have inalienable rights. These governments are checked by the rule of law, so that civil liberties are protected. They ensure freedom of conscience and freedom of expression, and ensure that men and women, homosexuals and heterosexuals, are entitled to equal treatment and protection under the law. And these governments have free-trade practices and an open market, and people may spend their recreational time as they wish.

The terrorists, and the Shari'a-based societies to which they aspire, have an entirely different philosophical point of view. Societies that espouse the following of Shari'a law, which is a code derived from a literalist reading of the Koran, are fundamentalist Islamists. They believe that people are born to serve Allah through a series of obligations that are prescribed in an ancient body of writings. These edicts vary from rituals of birth and funeral rites to the most intimate details of human life; they descend to the point of absurdity in matters such as how to blow your nose and with what foot to step into a bathroom. Humans in this philosophy must kill those among them who leave their faith, and are required to be hostile to people of other religions and ways of life. In their hostility, they are even sanctioned in the murder of innocent people. The edicts make no distinction between civilians and the military—anyone who does not share this faith is an infidel and can be marked for murder.

In this Shari'a society, women are subordinate to men. They must be confined to their houses, beaten if found disobedient, forced into marriage, and hidden behind the veil. The hands of thieves are cut off and capital punishment is performed on crowded public squares in front of cheering crowds. The terrorists seek to impose this way of life not only in Islamic countries, but, as Blair said, on Western societies too.

The central figure in this struggle is not Bin Laden, or Khomeini, or Hassan al-Banna, or Sayyid Qutb, but Muhammad. A premedieval figure to whom these four men—along with all faithful Muslims in our modern world—look for guidance, Muhammad and his teachings offer a fundamental challenge to the West. Faithful Muslims—all faithful Muslims—believe that they must emulate this man, in principle and practical matters, under all circumstances. And so, before we embark on a battle of ideas, we will need to take a look at this figure, and his presence in the daily lives and homes of faithful Muslims today.

On reading the Koran and the traditional writings, it is apparent that Muhammad's life not only provides rules for the daily lives of Muslims, it also demonstrates the means by which his values can be imposed. Yet remnants from some of the earliest Korans in existence, dating from the seventh and eighth centuries, show small aberrations from the text that is now considered the standard Koran. Nonetheless, just as some fundamentalist Christians cannot understand that the Bible went through numerous changes, interpretations, and translations before it became the contemporary text now widely used, and consider it inerrant, many fundamentalist Muslims consider the Koran a perfect, timeless representation of the unchanging word of God.

To spread his visions and teachings, which he believed to be from God, and to consolidate his secular power, Muhammad built the House of Islam using military tactics that included mass killing, torture, targeted assassination, lying, and the indiscriminate destruction of productive goods. This may be embarrassing, and even painful, for moderate Muslims to admit and to consider, but it is historical fact. And a close look at the propaganda produced by the terrorists reveals constant quotation of Muhammad's deeds and edicts to justify their actions and to call on other Muslims to support their cause.

In their thinking about radical Muslim terrorism, most politicians, journalists, intellectuals, and other commentators have avoided the core issue of the debate, which is Muhammad's example. In order to win the hearts and minds of those millions of undecided Muslims, it is crucial to engage them in a process of clear thinking on how to evaluate the moral guidance of the man whose compass they follow. The advantage of this rational process is that it provides an alternative to the utopia as well as the hell promised by the terrorists. Indeed, the threat of hell is the single most effective menace that the fundamentalists hold over the heads of young men and women in order to indoctrinate and intimidate them into violent action. Yet the literal translation of utopia is "not [a] place," from the Greek "ou," meaning not, or no, plus *topos*, meaning place. The dictionary defines a utopia as "an imaginary and indefinitely remote place." The true alternative to such an impossible place is the open society, democracy, which has already been empirically proven to work. The open society gives Muslims, as it gives Christians and Jews, the opportunity to liberate themselves from the ever-present menace of hell. The extremists tell the young people that they must defend their faith, avenge insults against Muhammad and the holy word of God, the Koran. What is it exactly that they think they are defending?

A call for clear thought on this important question should not be offensive, or hurtful, to Muslims. And yet many people in the West flinch from doing so. The *communis opinio* seems to hold that questioning or criticizing a holy figure is not polite behavior, somehow not done. This movement for cultural relativism within Western society betrays the basic values on which our open society is constructed. As thinking human beings, we should never censor our analytic thoughts; we should never censor our reason.

Along these lines, I would argue that Prime Minister Blair should rethink his bill against blasphemy. Years ago, some British Muslims unsuccessfully called for Salman Rushdie to be tried under Britain's blasphemy law after the publication of his controversial novel *The Satanic Verses*. But the law only recognized blasphemy against the Church of England, Britain's dominant, official religion. But in June 2005, the British parliament approved government plans to outlaw incitement to religious hatred. This bill was aimed primarily at preventing racism against Muslims in Britain. Even though the home secretary argued that the bill wasn't about stopping people from making jokes about religion—which would be a tragedy in the land that gave birth to Monty Python—or stopping people from having robust debates about religion, it is unclear why this bill was necessary. Inciting religious hatred is already against the law. And as the head of a civil rights group in Britain said, "In a democracy there is no right not to be offended." He added that religion is related to a body of ideas and people have the right to debate and criticize other people's ideas. Another activist fighting the bill averred, "The freedom to criticize ideas, any ideas—even if they are sincerely held beliefs—is one of the fundamental freedoms of society." As of this writing, the House of Lords has returned the bill to the House of Commons, saying it is a bad bill.

Muslims in Europe and across the world may be seen as roughly dividing into three groups. Most visible are the terrorists, who resort to violence (and their allies, the fundamentalists, who do not kill or maim, but provide the terrorists with material and nonmaterial or psychological assistance). Second, their polar opposite is group of people (and although tiny, it is growing) who may be characterized by its questioning of the relevance and moral soundness of Muhammad's example. They may one day provide an intellectual counterweight to the terrorists and their supporters. I, who was born and bred a Muslim, count myself among them. We in this group have embraced the open society as a true alternative to a society based on the laws of Muhammad—a better way to build a framework for human life. We could call this group the reformers.

The terrorists have far more power and resources than the reformers, but both groups vie to influence the thinking of the vast majority of Muslims. The reformers use only nonviolent means, like writing, to draw attention to debates over core values. The terrorists and fundamentalists, however, use force, the threat of force, appeals to pity ("look at what the West is doing to Islam and Muslims"), and ad hominem smears to evoke a knee-jerk community to withdraw into self-defense. In the West, these tactics give rise to moral relativists who defend so-called victims of Islamophobia; meanwhile, the reformists are shunned by their families and communities and live under the constant fear of assassination. In short, the core of the debate is made taboo, and the fundamentalists attain a near-monopoly on the hearts and minds of the third and largest group of Muslims, the undecided.

Who are these "undecided" Muslims? They are the group to which Tony Blair refers when he says, "The vast and overwhelming majority of Muslims here and abroad are decent and law-abiding people." They live in Edgware Road and Bradford, and in Amsterdam and Saint Denis; they are not fervent observers of every ritual of Islam, but they count themselves as believers. They are immigrants and second-generation youths who have come to the West to enjoy the benefits of the open society, in which they have a vested interest. But they do not question the infallibility of Muhammad and the soundness of his moral example. They know that Muhammad calls for slaughter of infidels; they know that the open society rightly condemns the slaughter of innocents. They are caught in a mental cramp of cognitive dissonance, and it is up to the West to support the reformists in trying to ease them out of that painful contradiction. The established Muslim organizations, which operate on government subsidy, offer no more than a cosmetic approach to eradicating terrorism inspired by the prophet Muhammad—"peace be upon Him," naturally.

The first victims of Muhammad are the minds of Muslims themselves. They are imprisoned in the fear of hell and so also fear the very natural pursuit of life, liberty, and happiness. There is as yet no consensus in the West on whether to support the side of the radical reformers. The present-day attitude of Western cultural relativists, who flinch from criticizing Muhammad for fear of offending Muslims, allow Western Muslims to hide from reviewing their own moral values. This attitude also betrays the tiny majority of Muslim reformers who desperately require the support—and even the physical protection—of their natural allies in the West.

Muslims must review and reform their approach to Muhammad's teachings if those who love freedom and the open society are to coexist peacefully with them. The terrorists and their allies the fundamentalists should not dictate to us Westerners the rules of the game. We must maintain and proclaim our core values of free and open debate, of rational thinking, and the rule of law not religion. In this, the resolve of the British people to preserve civil rights is brave, and should be an example to all of us. The use of torture and the denial of legal rights to suspects of terrorism will serve only to corrupt Western systems and views of the West as a model of openness. Such actions also provide the terrorists with facts that serve as ammunition to prove their specious argument that the West is hypocritical and morally confused.

Notes

———— ⟡ ————

CHAPTER ONE

3   *It is therefore not surprising:* NRC Handelsblad, July 8, 2002.

4   *Beating is degrading:* in the same article in the *NRC Handelsblad*, July 8, 2002.

5   *In a June 2002 interview:* in the *NRC Handelsblad*, July 8, 2002.

CHAPTER TWO

15   *Neither the Islam and Citizenship Society: Stichting Islam en Burgerschap.*

16   *Only aid organizations: Riagg.*

16   *The Child Welfare Council: Raad voor de Kinderbescherming.*

CHAPTER THREE

17   *The three main shortcomings:* listed in the United Nations' 2002–2003 *Arab Human Development Report.*

17   *Only about 330 foreign books: Stichting Speurwerk, Titelproductiestatistiek,* 1997.

17   *The United Nations reports: Trouw,* October 2, 2003.

22   *"Stay quietly in your homes":* Koran, Surah 33, verse 33 (Abdullah Yusuf Ali, translator).

22   *"And say to the believing women":* Surah 24, verse 31.

23   *"Oh Prophet!":* Surah 33, verse 59.

24   *The eleventh-century imam:* in his book *Wie luidt de doodsklok over de Arabieren?* (*Who Tolls the Bell for the Arabs?*), Marcel Kurpershoek.

25   *According to the Koran:* Koran, Surah 4, verse 34.

34   Customs and Morals in Islam: *Gewoontes en zeden in de Islam.*

34   Guide to Islamic Upbringing: *Gids tot de islamitische opvoeding.*

34   A Glimpse of Hell: *Een glimp van de hel.*

CHAPTER FOUR

35   *Nobody who has been following the debates:* The original version of this article appeared in the "Letter & Spirit" section of *Trouw* newspaper on March 16, 2002. Also published in *De zoontjesfabriek* (2002).

36   *The writer Leon de Winter:* In an article of November 10 in the "Letter & Spirit" section of *Trouw* newspaper.

37   *In addition, Muslims in Europe:* Marcel Kurpershoek (*NRC Handelsblad*, November 3).

41   *In the Netherlands and elsewhere in Europe:* Afshin Ellian.

CHAPTER FIVE

44   *This is "religion as a culture-forming factor":* T. von der Dunk, "De West en de Rest: over de gelijkwaardigheid van culturen ["The West and the Rest: On the Equality of Cultures"], in *Socialisme en Democratie*, vol. 58 no. 9, September 2001, pp. 391–399.

44   *In the year 2000 these Dutch communities:* All figures taken from *Integratie in het perspectief van immigratie* [*Integration from the perspective of immigration*]. Government Report, January 18, 2002, p. 66.

45   *Muslims now form the biggest ideological category:* Netherlands Scientific Council of Government Policy, *Nederland als immigratiesamenleving* [*The Netherlands as an immigration society*]. Reports for the government no. 60, The Hague, 2001.

45   *"The vast majority, especially those who come":* from economist Arie van der Zwan.

45   *"Their demographic profile is traditional":* A. van der Zwan, "Waar blijft de ombuiging in het immigratiebeleid?" ["When will immigration policy change"], in *Socialisme en Democratie*, vol. 59 no. 4, April 2002, pp. 43–54. See also: A. van der Zwan, "Alarmerende uitkomsten! De wrr-studie integratie van etnische minderheden" ["Alarming outcomes! The WRR think tank study on the integration of ethnic minorities"], in *Socialisme en Democratie*, vol. 58 no. 9, September 2001, pp. 421–425.

46   *Frank Bovenkerk and Yucel Yesilgöz:* F. Bovenkerk and Y. Yesilgöz, "Multiculturaliteit in de strafrechtpleging?" ["Multiculturalism in the administration of criminal justice?"], in *Tijdschrift voor Beleid, Politiek en Maatschappij* [*Periodical for Policy Politics and Society*], (1999) no. 4, p. 232.

46   *This is not surprising:* according to the two Italian researchers, Allievi and Castro, who attribute the lack of a deeper sociological analysis.

46   *There is also very little sociological research:* S. Allievi and F. Castro, "The Islamic presence in Italy: social rootedness and legal questions," in S. Ferrari and A. Bradney (eds.), *Islam and European Legal Systems*, Vermont, 2000, p. 198.

There seem to be no studies within the Islamic world of the sociogenesis and psychogenesis of Muslim culture, which are comparable to the work of the German sociologist Norbert Elias. On the basis of Elias's theory of civilization, the process of social integration can be described as the creation of, more or less, mutually dependent situations in an ever more complex society. The psychological component of this social change tends toward the development of steady and automatic self-control, which helps people with the growing demands of life. This increased self-control is shown by the fact that over the centuries European manners and morals have become more relaxed and refined. Initially social institutions imposed new codes of conduct, but over time this process became internalized. According to Elias, this trend began during the early Middle Ages, when—as they were forced to stay at the court—the free and independent knights gradually became dependent on the king. Here they learned to control their feelings and to be diplomatic. This court culture was at first imitated by the higher classes and spread to large sections of the population in the course of the twentieth century, following a big push for civilization. This did not just happen "of its own accord." Laborers and peasants were forced to adjust to the demands of a modern industrial society (through among other things, the introduction of compulsory military service and education, through having to learn the standard language, et cetera). N. Elias, *Het civilisatieproces: Sociogenetische en psychogenetische onderzoekingen* [The process of civilization: Socio-genetic and psycho-genetic investigations], Amsterdam, 2001 (1939).

47 *The Islamic identity (view of mankind and the world):* Pryce-Jones defines the specific concept of honor in the Islamic world as follows: "Honor is what makes life worthwhile: shame is a living death, not to be endured, requiring that it be avenged. Honor involves recognition, the openly acknowledged esteem of others which render a person secure and important in his or her own eyes and in front of everyone else. [. . .] Honor and its recognition set up the strongest possible patterns of conduct, in a hierarchy of deference and respect." (Pryce-Jones, *The closed circle*, 1989, p. 35).

48 *And marrying family members:* The recently published *Arab Human Development Report* evaluates the demographic situation in 22 Arab countries. The total population of these countries amounts to 280 million, of which 38 percent are between the ages of 0 and 14, and only 6 percent are over 60. The report offers two possible scenarios for the future until 2020. According to the first scenario, the Arab population will reach an estimated 459 million by 2020; the second predicts 410 million. UNDP, *Arab Human Development Report*, New York, 2002, p. 37.

48   *This premodern culture closely resembles:* which was developed by Jan Romein. Van der Loo and Van Reijen summarize the key elements of the GHP.

49   *Doing nothing is a luxury:* H. van der Loo and W. van Reijen, *Paradoxen van modernisering* [*Paradoxes of modernization*], Bussum, 1997, p. 70.

49   *The monotheism of Islam:* K. Armstrong, *Islam. Geschiedenis van een wereldgodsdients* [*History of a world religion*], Amsterdam, 2001, p. 58. See also: K. Armstrong, *Een Geschiedenis van God. Vierduizend jaar jodendom, christendom en islam* [A History of God. Four thousand years of Judaism, Christianity and Islam], Baarn, 1993.

49   *In* The Closed Circle: D. Pryce-Jones, *The closed circle.*

50   *The Muslims created a multiethnic:* Lewis, *What went wrong? The clash between Islam and modernity in the Middle-East,* Londen, 2002, p. 6.

51   *This all too simple response:* B. Lewis, *What went wrong?,* p. 158.

53   *According to the report:* UNDP, *Arab Human Development Report.*

54   *The result is a general stagnation:* H. Jansen, "Bush versus Bin Laden, het Western tegen de islam?" ["Bush versus Bin Laden, the West against Islam?"], in *International Spectator,* nr. 11, November 2001.

54   *There is corruption and apathy:* N. N. Ayubi, *Over-stating the Arab state: politics and society in the Middle-East,* New York, 1995, p. 125.

56   *If we define culture as the repertoire:* N. Wilterdink and B. van Heerikhuizen, *Samenlevingen: een verkenning van het terrein van de sociologi* [*Societies: an exploration of the sociologist's territory*], Groningen, 1993, p. 24.

58   *The Islamic world has seen little progress:* A. van der Zwan, "Waar blijft de ombuiging in het immigratiebeleid?"

59   *The group's disadvantages are considered:* P. de Beer, "PvdA moet terug naar de oorsprong" ["PvdA must return to its roots"], in *NRC Handelsblad* July 6, 2002.

61   *Galenkamp argued that this would be impossible:* M. Galenkamp, "Multiculturele samenleving in het geding" ["Multicultural society under discussion"], in *Justitiële Verkenningen* [*Judicial Explorations*], (2002) nr. 5.

63   *Referring to the study by the Netherlands:* Netherlands Scientific Council of Government Policy, *Nederland als immigratiesamenleving* [*The Netherlands as an immigration society*].

CHAPTER SIX

69   *In a Dutch newsmagazine:* HP/De Tijd Rob Oudkerk.

70   *If he really said to the Dutch weekly:* Vrij Nederland.

CHAPTER SEVEN

79 *Thou shalt have no other:* An interview by Arjan Visser as published in the series "The Ten Commandments" in the daily newspaper *Trouw.* "The Ten Commandments" is a series published in a daily newspaper in the Netherlands that interviews many prominent people following the format of the commandments. Copyright © 2003 Arjan Visser.

CHAPTER EIGHT

89 *"I notice that in your body":* This interview appeared on June 19, 2004, in the daily newspaper *Algemeen Dagblad,* with the help of Carine Damen.

CHAPTER NINE

95 *At times I end up:* This is the unabridged version of "Vrijheid verist permanent onderhoud" ["Freedom requires constant maintenance"] published on May 5, 2003, in the daily newspaper *NRC Handelsblad.*

CHAPTER ELEVEN

113 *An average of eighty women:* This is a reedited version of the article published in *NRC Handelsblad* daily newspaper, October 3, 2003. It is also included in *De Maagdenkooi* [*The Virgins' Cage*], 2004.

CHAPTER TWELVE

119 *Genital mutilation of girls:* This chapter is based on the article "Besnijdenis mag niet worden gedoogd" ["Circumcision must not be tolerated"], published in the daily newspaper *de Volkskrant,* February 7, 2004.

119 *Since the birth of a stillborn child:* From the article by Steffie Kouters in the *Volkskrant* magazine, July 10, 2004.

120 *According to a story in the* New York Times: by Sharon LaFraniere, September 28, 2005.

121 *A medical report for the government:* "Strategies for the prevention of circumcision in girls. Assessment and recommendations, of the Vrije Universiteit [VU] Medical Center in Amsterdam (October 2003).

CHAPTER THIRTEEN

129 *Since the early 1900s:* Ten tips for Muslim women who want to leave, originally published in *De maagdenkooi* [*The Virgins' Cage*] (2004).

CHAPTER FIFTEEN

151 *My parents brought me up:* This is the unabridged version of the article that appeared on October 30, 2004, in the daily newspaper *De Volkskrant.*

157 *These are the words of Mohamed Sini:* quoted in the daily newspaper *De Volks-krant.*

157 *"I'm not going to waste my time":* De Volkskrant

158 *"They simply don't deserve a reaction"* from the Dutch daily newspaper *Trouw.*

158 *The chairman of the Turkish Muslim organization:* het Rottersdam Dagblad

159 *Yet the regional institutes for mental welfare:* the psychiatrist Carla Rus points out in articles in two Dutch newspapers, *Trouw* and *De Volkskrant.*

Index